Ninja Dual Zone Air Fryer

Cookbook for UK

Quick, Easy and Crispy Recipes Ready in Less Than 30 Minutes, Double the Flavor for a Convenient and Economical Solution for Busy People

Rhys Gallagher

CONTENTS

INTRODUCTION I

Unveiling the Innovative Features of a Dual Zone Air Fryer II
Embracing the Health-Boosting Benefits of Air Fryers II
Unlocking the Secrets to Maximizing Your Air Fryer's Potential III

Measurement Conversions IV

Breakfast Recipes 6

Air Fried Bacon And Eggs 6
Spinach Egg Muffins 6
Cinnamon Apple French Toast 6
Pumpkin French Toast Casserole With Sweet And Spicy Twisted Bacon 6
Breakfast Bacon 7
Breakfast Sausage Omelet 7
Egg White Muffins 7
Cornbread 8
Egg And Avocado In The Ninja Foodi 8
Banana Muffins 8
Baked Mushroom And Mozzarella Frittata With Breakfast Potatoes 9
Cheesy Baked Eggs 9
Healthy Oatmeal Muffins 10
Spinach And Red Pepper Egg Cups With Coffee-glazed Canadian Bacon 10
Quiche Breakfast Peppers 10
Banana And Raisins Muffins 11
Sausage & Butternut Squash 11
Sweet Potato Hash 11
Brussels Sprouts Potato Hash 12
Egg With Baby Spinach 12
Sausage Hash And Baked Eggs 12
Morning Egg Rolls 13
Breakfast Cheese Sandwich 13
Air Fryer Sausage Patties 14
Bagels 14

Snacks And Appetizers Recipes 15

Crispy Plantain Chips 15
Peppered Asparagus 15
Roasted Tomato Bruschetta With Toasty Garlic Bread.......................................15
Chicken Tenders 16
Stuffed Mushrooms 16
Garlic Bread..16
Crab Cakes...17
Stuffed Bell Peppers 17
Parmesan French Fries 17
Fried Pickles 17
Zucchini Chips 18
Miso-glazed Shishito Peppers Charred Lemon Shishito Peppers 18
Beef Jerky Pineapple Jerky 18
Mozzarella Balls 19
Cheese Stuffed Mushrooms 19
Potato Chips 19
Cheese Corn Fritters 20
Mac And Cheese Balls 20
Strawberries And Walnuts Muffins..20
Crab Cake Poppers 21
Fried Cheese 21
Avocado Fries With Sriracha Dip..21
Cheddar Quiche 22
Chili-lime Crispy Chickpeas Pizza-seasoned Crispy Chickpeas 22
Tater Tots 22

Poultry Recipes...23

Yummy Chicken Breasts 23
Glazed Thighs With French Fries 23
Chicken Leg Piece..23
General Tso's Chicken..24
Crispy Sesame Chicken 24
"fried" Chicken With Warm Baked Potato Salad...25
Chicken & Broccoli 25
Whole Chicken 26
Cheddar-stuffed Chicken 26
Chicken And Potatoes 26
Easy Chicken Thighs 27
Almond Chicken 27
Barbecue Chicken Drumsticks With Crispy Kale Chips.......................................27
Chicken Thighs With Brussels Sprouts 28

Chicken Wings..28
Crumbed Chicken Katsu..28
Chicken Breast Strips...29
Pretzel Chicken Cordon Bleu 29
Chicken Caprese..29
Cornish Hen With Asparagus 30
Balsamic Duck Breast 30
Chicken Potatoes 30
Roasted Garlic Chicken Pizza With Cauliflower "wings" 31
Buffalo Chicken 31
Chicken Cordon Bleu...32

Beef, Pork, And Lamb Recipes 33

Korean Bbq Beef 33
Bell Peppers With Sausages 33
Air Fryer Meatloaves 33
Beef Kofta Kebab 34
Beef Ribs Ii 34
Chinese Bbq Pork..34
Air Fried Lamb Chops 35
Pork Chops..35
Steak In Air Fry 35
Tomahawk Steak 35
Pork Chops And Potatoes 36
Beef Ribs I...36
Pork Chops With Brussels Sprouts 36
Turkey And Beef Meatballs...37
Italian-style Meatballs With Garlicky Roasted Broccoli........................37
Beef And Bean Taquitos With Mexican Rice 38
Breaded Pork Chops 38
Pork Chops With Apples...38
Mongolian Beef With Sweet Chili Brussels Sprouts 39
Tender Pork Chops...39
Tasty Pork Skewers 40
Tasty Lamb Patties 40
Lamb Chops With Dijon Garlic 40
Steak And Asparagus Bundles 41
Garlic Sirloin Steak 41

Fish And Seafood Recipes 42

Bang Bang Shrimp 42
Glazed Scallops...42

Broiled Crab Cakes With Hush Puppies...42
Salmon With Coconut..43
Spicy Salmon Fillets 43
Salmon Nuggets...43
Crusted Shrimp...44
Herb Tuna Patties...44
Beer Battered Fish Fillet...44
Scallops With Greens..45
Smoked Salmon 45
Crumb-topped Sole 45
Broiled Teriyaki Salmon With Eggplant In Stir-fry Sauce..46
Parmesan-crusted Fish Sticks With Baked Macaroni And Cheese.....................................46
Garlic Shrimp With Pasta Alfredo..47
Salmon With Fennel Salad..47
Fried Tilapia...48
Keto Baked Salmon With Pesto..48
Chili Lime Tilapia...48
Savory Salmon Fillets...48
Honey Sriracha Mahi Mahi...49
Fried Lobster Tails..49
Seafood Shrimp Omelet..49
Codfish With Herb Vinaigrette...50
Frozen Breaded Fish Fillet..50

Vegetables And Sides Recipes

Vegetables And Sides Recipes...51
Buffalo Seitan With Crispy Zucchini Noodles 51
Mixed Air Fry Veggies..51
Fresh Mix Veggies In Air Fryer 52
Air Fryer Vegetables...52
Acorn Squash Slices 52
Rosemary Asparagus & Potatoes..53
Fried Asparagus 53
Fried Artichoke Hearts 53
Chickpea Fritters 53
Potatoes & Beans..54
Pepper Poppers...54
Healthy Air Fried Veggies 54
Brussels Sprouts..55
Fried Olives 55
Fried Patty Pan Squash...55
Garlic-rosemary Brussels Sprouts...56
Saucy Carrots..56
Quinoa Patties..56

Herb And Lemon Cauliflower...57
Delicious Potatoes & Carrots..57
Green Beans With Baked Potatoes...57
Cheesy Potatoes With Asparagus...58
Balsamic-glazed Tofu With Roasted Butternut Squash...58
Bacon Wrapped Corn Cob..59
Sweet Potatoes & Brussels Sprouts...59

Desserts Recipes 60

S'mores Dip With Cinnamon-sugar Tortillas...60
Lemony Sweet Twists...60
Oreo Rolls..60
Baked Apples..61
Victoria Sponge Cake...61
Apple Hand Pies...61
Chocó Lava Cake..62
Fried Oreos...62
Brownie Muffins..62
Apple Crisp...63
Dessert Empanadas..63
Chocolate Chip Cake..63
Chocolate Cookies 64
Apple Fritters 64
Strawberry Shortcake...64
Fudge Brownies..65
Walnut Baklava Bites Pistachio Baklava Bites 65
Cinnamon Sugar Dessert Fries 66
Zesty Cranberry Scones...66
Air Fryer Sweet Twists..66
Blueberry Pie Egg Rolls..67
Grilled Peaches 67
Delicious Apple Fritters...67
Biscuit Doughnuts...68
Bread Pudding...68

Appendix : Recipes Index 69

INTRODUCTION

Rhys Gallagher, an internationally acclaimed chef known for his exquisite fusion of classic and contemporary techniques, unveils the magic of the Ninja Dual Zone Air Fryer in a manner that's both enlightening and captivating. Through this cookbook, he invites every home cook, beginner or seasoned, to embark on a culinary voyage that transcends the boundaries of traditional cooking.

The Ninja Dual Zone Air Fryer, with its cutting-edge dual cooking zones and precision controls, serves as the canvas for Gallagher's culinary masterpieces. What makes this cookbook stand out is the seamless blend of Rhys's culinary wisdom with the technological prowess of the air fryer. This partnership aims to reinvent the way we perceive air frying, revealing its potential not just as a healthier alternative, but as a tool for gourmet artistry.

With dishes that span continents, from the aromatic streets of Asia to the rustic heart of Mediterranean villages, Gallagher's recipes explore the versatility of the air fryer. Each page exudes passion, revealing secrets to creating dishes that are both nourishing for the body and soul-satisfying.

But beyond the recipes, Rhys Gallagher's "Ninja Dual Zone Air Fryer Cookbook" is a journey of discovery. It's about unearthing the potential within, harnessing the power of modern technology, and realizing that the heart of culinary excellence lies in understanding and respect – for ingredients, for tools, and for the diners we serve.

Whether you're looking to recreate the charm of age-old family recipes or venture into new gastronomic territories, this cookbook is your guiding star. It's not just about using the Ninja Dual Zone Air Fryer; it's about transforming every meal into an occasion, every dish into a story, and every bite into a memory.

Join Rhys Gallagher on this culinary expedition and let the "Ninja Dual Zone Air Fryer Cookbook" redefine your kitchen narrative, turning every meal into a gourmet experience, every day into a feast, and every moment into a celebration of taste.

Unveiling the Innovative Features of a Dual Zone Air Fryer

Two Independent Cooking Zones

Cook two different dishes simultaneously, each with separate temperature and time settings. Perfect for multi-course meals or accommodating varied taste preferences.

Enhanced Capacity

With two cooking compartments, the Dual Zone Air Fryer offers more cooking space, ideal for larger families or entertaining guests.

Versatile Cooking Functions

Beyond frying, this appliance may include options for baking, roasting, grilling, and dehydrating, offering multifunctional convenience.

Health-Focused Cooking

As with other Air Fryers, the Dual Zone model emphasizes cooking with minimal or no oil, promoting a healthier approach to favorite fried foods.

Easy Maintenance

Often constructed with non-stick materials and dishwasher-safe parts, cleaning becomes a breeze, making daily use more practical.

Energy Efficiency

By cooking two dishes simultaneously, this Air Fryer can save energy and reduce overall cooking time.

Embracing the Health-Boosting Benefits of Air Fryers

- **Reduced Fat Content**

Air Fryers cook food by circulating hot air around it, requiring little to no oil. This can significantly reduce the fat content of many dishes, especially when compared to traditional deep frying.

- **Lower Calorie Intake**

By minimizing the use of oil, air-fried foods often contain fewer calories, supporting weight management and overall wellness.

- **Retention of Nutrients**

Cooking at precise temperatures with an Air Fryer may help in retaining more vitamins and minerals in food, preserving nutritional value.

- **Elimination of Harmful Compounds**

Traditional frying at high temperatures can lead to the formation of harmful compounds like acrylamide. Air frying can reduce or eliminate the production of these substances.

- **Support for Special Diets**

Air Fryers offer control and consistency in cooking, making it easier to prepare meals that comply with specific dietary needs, such as gluten-free or low-sodium diets.

- **Reduced Risk of Diseases**

By aiding in the reduction of unhealthy fats and harmful compounds, air frying can contribute to a heart-healthy diet and potentially lower the risk of certain chronic diseases.

- **Versatility for Healthier Choices**

Air Fryers aren't limited to frying. They can also roast, grill, and bake, encouraging the incorporation of a wider variety of wholesome foods into the diet.

- **Less Use of Processed Oils**

Air frying allows for the choice of healthier oils or even the complete omission of oil, reducing the consumption of processed or saturated fats.

- **Improved Food Texture**

Air frying provides a crispy texture without the need for deep frying, offering a satisfying experience for those craving crunchy foods without the added fat.

Unlocking the Secrets to Maximizing Your Air Fryer's Potential

Preheat When Necessary: For some recipes, preheating the Air Fryer can lead to better results. Check the instruction manual or recipe guidelines to determine when preheating is recommended.

Don't Overcrowd: Overcrowding can lead to uneven cooking. Cook in batches if necessary to ensure proper air circulation and consistent results.

Shake or Flip as Needed: For some foods, shaking or flipping partway through cooking ensures even crispiness. Follow the recipe instructions or use your judgment for best results.

Use Healthy Oils: If a recipe calls for oil, choose healthier options like olive or avocado oil. A simple oil mister can help you apply it evenly without overdoing it.

Keep It Clean: Regular cleaning preserves the functionality and longevity of the Air Fryer. Follow the manufacturer's guidelines for cleaning, and make sure to tackle any food residue promptly.

Have Fun and Be Creative: Finally, let your creativity shine. Experiment with flavors, textures, and ingredients. The Air Fryer is a tool that invites culinary exploration, so enjoy the process!

Measurement Conversions

BASIC KITCHEN CONVERSIONS & EQUIVALENTS

DRY MEASUREMENTS CONVERSION CHART

3 TEASPOONS = 1 TABLESPOON = 1/16 CUP

6 TEASPOONS = 2 TABLESPOONS = 1/8 CUP

12 TEASPOONS = 4 TABLESPOONS = 1/4 CUP

24 TEASPOONS = 8 TABLESPOONS = 1/2 CUP

36 TEASPOONS = 12 TABLESPOONS = 3/4 CUP

48 TEASPOONS = 16 TABLESPOONS = 1 CUP

METRIC TO US COOKING CONVERSIONS

OVEN TEMPERATURES

120 °C = 250 °F

160 °C = 320 °F

180° C = 350 °F

205 °C = 400 °F

220 °C = 425 °F

LIQUID MEASUREMENTS CONVERSION CHART

8 FLUID OUNCES = 1 CUP = 1/2 PINT = 1/4 QUART

16 FLUID OUNCES = 2 CUPS = 1 PINT = 1/2 QUART

32 FLUID OUNCES = 4 CUPS = 2 PINTS = 1 QUART

= 1/4 GALLON

128 FLUID OUNCES = 16 CUPS = 8 PINTS = 4 QUARTS = 1 GALLON

BAKING IN GRAMS

1 CUP FLOUR = 140 GRAMS

1 CUP SUGAR = 150 GRAMS

1 CUP POWDERED SUGAR = 160 GRAMS

1 CUP HEAVY CREAM = 235 GRAMS

VOLUME

1 MILLILITER = 1/5 TEASPOON

5 ML = 1 TEASPOON

15 ML = 1 TABLESPOON

240 ML = 1 CUP OR 8 FLUID OUNCES

1 LITER = 34 FL. OUNCES

WEIGHT

1 GRAM = .035 OUNCES

100 GRAMS = 3.5 OUNCES

500 GRAMS = 1.1 POUNDS

1 KILOGRAM = 35 OUNCES

US TO METRIC COOKING CONVERSIONS

1/5 TSP = 1 ML

1 TSP = 5 ML

1 TBSP = 15 ML

1 FL OUNCE = 30 ML

1 CUP = 237 ML

1 PINT (2 CUPS) = 473 ML

1 QUART (4 CUPS) = .95 LITER

1 GALLON (16 CUPS) = 3.8 LITERS

1 OZ = 28 GRAMS

1 POUND = 454 GRAMS

BUTTER

1 CUP BUTTER = 2 STICKS = 8 OUNCES = 230 GRAMS = 8 TABLESPOONS

WHAT DOES 1 CUP EQUAL

1 CUP = 8 FLUID OUNCES

1 CUP = 16 TABLESPOONS

1 CUP = 48 TEASPOONS

1 CUP = 1/2 PINT

1 CUP = 1/4 QUART

1 CUP = 1/16 GALLON

1 CUP = 240 ML

BAKING PAN CONVERSIONS

1 CUP ALL-PURPOSE FLOUR = 4.5 OZ

1 CUP ROLLED OATS = 3 OZ 1 LARGE EGG = 1.7 OZ

1 CUP BUTTER = 8 OZ 1 CUP MILK = 8 OZ

1 CUP HEAVY CREAM = 8.4 OZ

1 CUP GRANULATED SUGAR = 7.1 OZ

1 CUP PACKED BROWN SUGAR = 7.75 OZ

1 CUP VEGETABLE OIL = 7.7 OZ

1 CUP UNSIFTED POWDERED SUGAR = 4.4 OZ

BAKING PAN CONVERSIONS

9-INCH ROUND CAKE PAN = 12 CUPS

10-INCH TUBE PAN =16 CUPS

11-INCH BUNDT PAN = 12 CUPS

9-INCH SPRINGFORM PAN = 10 CUPS

9 X 5 INCH LOAF PAN = 8 CUPS

9-INCH SQUARE PAN = 8 CUPS

Breakfast Recipes

Air Fried Bacon And Eggs

Servings: 1
Cooking Time: 10 Minutes
Ingredients:

- 2 eggs
- 2 slices bacon

Directions:

1. Grease a ramekin using cooking spray.
2. Install the crisper plate in the zone 1 drawer and place the bacon inside it. Insert the drawer into the unit.
3. Crack the eggs and add them to the greased ramekin.
4. Install the crisper plate in the zone 2 drawer and place the ramekin inside it. Insert the drawer into the unit.
5. Select zone 1 to AIR FRY for 9–11 minutes at 400 degrees F/ 200 degrees C. Select zone 2 to AIR FRY for 8–9 minutes at 350 degrees F/ 175 degrees C. Press SYNC.
6. Press START/STOP to begin cooking.
7. Enjoy!

Nutrition Info:

- (Per serving) Calories 331 | Fat 24.5g | Sodium 1001mg | Carbs 1.2g | Fiber 0g | Sugar 0.7g | Protein 25.3g

Spinach Egg Muffins

Servings: 4
Cooking Time: 13 Minutes.
Ingredients:

- 4 tablespoons milk
- 4 tablespoons frozen spinach, thawed
- 4 large eggs
- 8 teaspoons grated cheese
- Salt, to taste
- Black pepper, to taste
- Cooking Spray

Directions:

1. Grease four small-sized ramekin with cooking spray.
2. Add egg, cheese, spinach, and milk to a bowl and beat well.
3. Divide the mixture into the four small ramekins and top them with salt and black pepper.
4. Place the two ramekins in each of the two crisper plate.
5. Return the crisper plate to the Ninja Foodi Dual Zone Air Fryer.
6. Choose the Air Fry mode for Zone 1 and set the temperature to 390 degrees F and the time to 13 minutes.
7. Select the "MATCH" button to copy the settings for Zone 2.
8. Initiate cooking by pressing the START/STOP button.

9. Serve warm.
Nutrition Info:

- (Per serving) Calories 237 | Fat 19g |Sodium 518mg | Carbs 7g | Fiber 1.5g | Sugar 3.4g | Protein 12g

Cinnamon Apple French Toast

Servings: 8
Cooking Time: 10 Minutes
Ingredients:

- 1 egg, lightly beaten
- 4 bread slices
- 1 tbsp cinnamon
- 15ml milk
- 23ml maple syrup
- 45 ml applesauce

Directions:

1. In a bowl, whisk egg, milk, cinnamon, applesauce, and maple syrup.
2. Insert a crisper plate in the Ninja Foodi air fryer baskets.
3. Dip each slice in egg mixture and place in both baskets.
4. Select zone 1 then select "air fry" mode and set the temperature to 355 degrees F for 10 minutes. Press "match" to match zone 2 settings to zone 1. Press "start/stop" to begin.

Nutrition Info:

- (Per serving) Calories 64 | Fat 1.5g |Sodium 79mg | Carbs 10.8g | Fiber 1.3g | Sugar 4.8g | Protein 2.3g

Pumpkin French Toast Casserole With Sweet And Spicy Twisted Bacon

Servings:4
Cooking Time: 35 Minutes
Ingredients:

- FOR THE FRENCH TOAST CASSEROLE
- 3 large eggs
- 1 cup unsweetened almond milk
- 1 cup canned unsweetened pumpkin puree
- 2 teaspoons pumpkin pie spice
- ¼ cup packed light brown sugar
- 1 teaspoon vanilla extract
- 6 cups French bread cubes
- 1 teaspoon vegetable oil
- ¼ cup maple syrup
- FOR THE BACON
- 2 tablespoons light brown sugar
- ⅛ teaspoon cayenne pepper
- 8 slices bacon

Directions:

1. To prep the French toast casserole: In a shallow bowl, whisk together the eggs, almond milk, pumpkin puree, pumpkin pie spice, brown sugar, and vanilla.

2. Add the bread cubes to the egg mixture, making sure the bread is fully coated in the custard. Let sit for at least 10 minutes to allow the bread to soak up the custard.

3. To prep the bacon: In a small bowl, combine the brown sugar and cayenne.

4. Arrange the bacon on a cutting board in a single layer. Evenly sprinkle the strips with the brown sugar mixture. Fold the bacon strip in half lengthwise. Hold one end of the bacon steady and twist the other end so the bacon resembles a straw.

5. To cook the casserole and bacon: Brush the Zone 1 basket with the oil. Pour the French toast casserole into the Zone 1 basket, drizzle with maple syrup, and insert the basket in the unit. Install a crisper plate in the Zone 2 basket, add the bacon twists in a single layer, and insert the basket in the unit. For the best fit, arrange the bacon twists across the unit, front to back.

6. Select Zone 1, select BAKE, set the temperature to 330°F, and set the time to 35 minutes.

7. Select Zone 2, select AIR FRY, set the temperature to 400°F, and set the time to 12 minutes. Select SMART FINISH.

8. Press START/PAUSE to begin cooking.

9. When cooking is complete, transfer the bacon to a plate lined with paper towels. Let cool for 2 to 3 minutes before serving with the French toast casserole.

Nutrition Info:
- (Per serving) Calories: 601; Total fat: 28g; Saturated fat: 9g; Carbohydrates: 67g; Fiber: 2.5g; Protein: 17g; Sodium: 814mg

Breakfast Bacon

Servings: 4
Cooking Time: 14 Minutes.
Ingredients:
- ½ lb. bacon slices

Directions:
1. Spread half of the bacon slices in each of the crisper plate evenly in a single layer.

2. Return the crisper plate to the Ninja Foodi Dual Zone Air Fryer.

3. Choose the Air Fry mode for Zone 1 and set the temperature to 390 degrees F and the time to 14 minutes.

4. Select the "MATCH" button to copy the settings for Zone 2.

5. Initiate cooking by pressing the START/STOP button.

6. Flip the crispy bacon once cooked halfway through, then resume cooking.

7. Serve.

Nutrition Info:

- (Per serving) Calories 273 | Fat 22g |Sodium 517mg | Carbs 3.3g | Fiber 0.2g | Sugar 1.4g | Protein 16.1g

Breakfast Sausage Omelet

Servings:2
Cooking Time:8
Ingredients:
- ¼ pound breakfast sausage, cooked and crumbled
- 4 eggs, beaten
- ½ cup pepper Jack cheese blend
- 2 tablespoons green bell pepper, sliced
- 1 green onion, chopped
- 1 pinch cayenne pepper
- Cooking spray

Directions:
1. Take a bowl and whisk eggs in it along with crumbled sausage, pepper Jack cheese, green onions, red bell pepper, and cayenne pepper.

2. Mix it all well.

3. Take two cake pans that fit inside the air fryer and grease it with oil spray.

4. Divide the omelet mixture between cake pans.

5. Put the cake pans inside both of the Ninja Foodie 2-Basket Air Fryer baskets.

6. Turn on the BAKE function of the zone 1 basket and let it cook for 15-20 minutes at 310 degrees F.

7. Select MATCH button for zone 2 basket.

8. Once the cooking cycle completes, take out, and serve hot, as a delicious breakfast.

Nutrition Info:
- (Per serving) Calories 691| Fat52.4g | Sodium1122 mg | Carbs 13.3g | Fiber 1.8g| Sugar 7g | Protein 42g

Egg White Muffins

Servings: 8
Cooking Time: 10 Minutes
Ingredients:
- 4 slices center-cut bacon, cut into strips
- 4 ounces baby bella mushrooms, roughly chopped
- 2 ounces sun-dried tomatoes
- 2 tablespoon sliced black olives
- 2 tablespoons grated or shredded parmesan
- 2 tablespoons shredded mozzarella
- ¼ teaspoon black pepper
- ¾ cup liquid egg whites
- 2 tablespoons liquid egg whites

Directions:
1. Heat a saucepan with a little oil, add the bacon and mushrooms and cook until fully cooked and crispy, about 6–8 minutes.

2. While the bacon and mushrooms cook, mix the ¾ cup liquid egg whites, sun-dried tomato, olives, parmesan, mozzarella, and black pepper together in a large bowl.

3. Add the cooked bacon and mushrooms to the tomato and olive mixture, stirring everything together.

4. Spoon the mixture into muffin molds, followed by 2 tablespoons of egg whites over the top.

5. Place half the muffins mold in zone 1 and half in zone 2, then insert the drawers into the unit.

6. Select zone 1, select AIR FRY, set temperature to 390 degrees F/ 200 degrees C, and set time to 22 minutes.

7. Select MATCH to match zone 2 settings to zone 1. Press the START/STOP button to begin cooking.

8. When cooking is complete, remove the molds and enjoy!

Nutrition Info:

- (Per serving) Calories 104 | Fat 5.6g   Sodium 269mg | Carbs 3.5g | Fiber 0.8g | Sugar 0.3g | Protein 10.3g

Cornbread

Servings: 6
Cooking Time: 15 Minutes

Ingredients:

- 1 cup cornmeal
- 1 cup all-purpose flour
- 1 tablespoon sugar
- 2 teaspoons baking powder
- ½ teaspoon baking soda
- ½ teaspoon salt
- 1 stick butter melted
- 1½ cups buttermilk
- 2 eggs
- 113g diced chiles

Directions:

1. Mix cornmeal with flour, sugar, baking powder, baking soda, salt, butter, milk, eggs and chiles in a bowl until smooth.

2. Spread this mixture in two greased 4-inch baking pans.

3. Place one pan in each air fryer basket.

4. Return the air fryer basket 1 to Zone 1, and basket 2 to Zone 2 of the Ninja Foodi 2-Basket Air Fryer.

5. Choose the "Air Fry" mode for Zone 1 at 330 degrees F and 15 minutes of cooking time.

6. Select the "MATCH COOK" option to copy the settings for Zone 2.

7. Initiate cooking by pressing the START/PAUSE BUTTON.

8. Slice and serve.

Nutrition Info:

- (Per serving) Calories 199 | Fat 11.1g |Sodium 297mg | Carbs 14.9g | Fiber 1g | Sugar 2.5g | Protein 9.9g

Egg And Avocado In The Ninja Foodi

Servings:2
Cooking Time:12

Ingredients:

- 2 Avocados, pitted and cut in half
- Garlic salt, to taste
- Cooking for greasing
- 4 eggs
- ¼ teaspoon of Paprika powder, for sprinkling
- 1/3 cup parmesan cheese, crumbled
- 6 bacon strips, raw

Directions:

1. First cut the avocado in half and pit it.

2. Now scoop out the flesh from the avocado and keep intact some of it

3. Crack one egg in each hole of avocado and sprinkle paprika and garlic salt

4. Top it with cheese at the end.

5. Now put it into tin foils and then put it in the air fryer zone basket 1

6. Put bacon strips in zone 2 basket.

7. Now for zone 1, set it to AIR FRY mode at 350 degrees F for 10 minutes

8. And for zone 2, set it 400 degrees for 12 minutes AIR FRY mode.

9. Press the Smart finish button and press start, it will finish both at the same time.

10. Once done, serve and enjoy.

Nutrition Info:

- (Per serving) Calories609 | Fat53.2g | Sodium 335mg | Carbs 18.1g | Fiber13.5g | Sugar 1.7g | Protein 21.3g

Banana Muffins

Servings: 10
Cooking Time: 15 Minutes

Ingredients:

- 2 very ripe bananas
- ⅓ cup olive oil
- 1 egg
- ½ cup brown sugar
- 1 teaspoon vanilla extract
- 1 teaspoon cinnamon
- ¾ cup self-rising flour

Directions:

1. In a large mixing bowl, mash the bananas, then add the egg, brown sugar, olive oil, and vanilla. To blend, stir everything together thoroughly.

2. Fold in the flour and cinnamon until everything is just blended.

3. Fill muffin molds evenly with the mixture (silicone or paper).

4. Install a crisper plate in both drawers. Place the muffin molds in a single layer in each drawer. Insert the drawers into the unit.

5. Select zone 1, select AIR FRY, set temperature to 360 degrees F/ 180 degrees C, and set time to 15 minutes. Select MATCH to match zone 2 settings to zone 1. Select START/STOP to begin.

6. Once the timer has finished, remove the muffins from the drawers.

7. Serve and enjoy!

Nutrition Info:

• (Per serving) Calories 148 | Fat 7.3g | Sodium 9mg | Carbs 19.8g | Fiber 1g | Sugar 10g | Protein 1.8g

Baked Mushroom And Mozzarella Frittata With Breakfast Potatoes

Servings:4

Cooking Time: 35 Minutes

Ingredients:

• FOR THE FRITTATA

• 8 large eggs

• ⅓ cup whole milk

• 1 teaspoon kosher salt

• ½ teaspoon freshly ground black pepper

• 1 cup sliced cremini mushrooms (about 2 ounces)

• 1 teaspoon olive oil

• 2 ounces part-skim mozzarella cheese, cut into ½-inch cubes

• FOR THE POTATOES

• 2 russet potatoes, cut into ½-inch cubes

• 1 tablespoon olive oil

• ½ teaspoon garlic powder

• ¼ teaspoon kosher salt

• ¼ teaspoon freshly ground black pepper

Directions:

1. To prep the frittata: In a large bowl, whisk together the eggs, milk, salt, and pepper. Stir in the mushrooms.

2. To prep the potatoes: In a large bowl, combine the potatoes, olive oil, garlic powder, salt, and black pepper.

3. To cook the frittata and potatoes: Brush the bottom of the Zone 1 basket with 1 teaspoon of olive oil. Add the egg mixture to the basket, top with the mozzarella cubes, and insert the basket in the unit. Install a crisper plate in the Zone 2 basket. Place the potatoes in the basket and insert the basket in the unit.

4. Select Zone 1, select BAKE, set the temperature to 350°F, and set the time to 30 minutes.

5. Select Zone 2, select AIR FRY, set the temperature to 400°F, and set the time to 35 minutes. Select SMART FINISH.

6. Press START/PAUSE to begin cooking.

7. When the Zone 2 timer reads 15 minutes, press START/PAUSE. Remove the basket and shake the potatoes for 10 seconds. Reinsert the basket and press START/PAUSE to resume cooking.

8. When cooking is complete, the frittata will pull away from the edges of the basket and the potatoes will be golden brown. Transfer the frittata to a cutting board and cut into 4 portions. Serve with the potatoes.

Nutrition Info:

• (Per serving) Calories: 307; Total fat: 17g; Saturated fat: 5.5g; Carbohydrates: 18g; Fiber: 1g; Protein: 19g; Sodium: 600mg

Cheesy Baked Eggs

Servings: 4

Cooking Time: 16 Minutes

Ingredients:

• 4 large eggs

• 57g smoked gouda, shredded

• Everything bagel seasoning, to taste

• Salt and pepper to taste

Directions:

1. Crack one egg in each ramekin.

2. Top the egg with bagel seasoning, black pepper, salt and gouda.

3. Place 2 ramekins in each air fryer basket.

4. Return the air fryer basket 1 to Zone 1, and basket 2 to Zone 2 of the Ninja Foodi 2-Basket Air Fryer.

5. Choose the "Air Fry" mode for Zone 1 and set the temperature to 400 degrees F and 16 minutes of cooking time.

6. Select the "MATCH COOK" option to copy the settings for Zone 2.

7. Initiate cooking by pressing the START/PAUSE BUTTON.

8. Serve warm.

Nutrition Info:

• (Per serving) Calories 190 | Fat 18g |Sodium 150mg | Carbs 0.6g | Fiber 0.4g | Sugar 0.4g | Protein 7.2g

Healthy Oatmeal Muffins

Servings: 6
Cooking Time: 17 Minutes
Ingredients:

- 1 egg
- ¼ tsp ground ginger
- 1 tsp ground cinnamon
- ½ tsp baking soda
- ½ tsp baking powder
- 55g brown sugar
- ½ tsp vanilla
- 2 tbsp butter, melted
- 125g applesauce
- 61ml milk
- 68gm whole wheat flour
- 100gm quick oats
- Pinch of salt

Directions:

1. In a mixing bowl, mix together all dry the ingredients.
2. In a separate bowl, add the remaining ingredients and mix well.
3. Add the dry ingredients mixture into the wet mixture and mix until well combined.
4. Pour the batter into the silicone muffin moulds.
5. Insert a crisper plate in the Ninja Foodi air fryer baskets.
6. Place muffin moulds in both baskets.
7. Select zone 1 then select "bake" mode and set the temperature to 390 degrees F for 17 minutes. Press "start/stop" to begin.

Nutrition Info:

- (Per serving) Calories 173 | Fat 5.8g |Sodium 177mg | Carbs 26.6g | Fiber 2.1g | Sugar 8.7g | Protein 4.2g

Spinach And Red Pepper Egg Cups With Coffee-glazed Canadian Bacon

Servings:6
Cooking Time: 13 Minutes
Ingredients:

- FOR THE EGG CUPS
- 4 large eggs
- ¼ cup heavy (whipping) cream
- ¼ teaspoon kosher salt
- ¼ teaspoon freshly ground black pepper
- ½ cup roasted red peppers (about 1 whole pepper), drained and chopped
- ½ cup baby spinach, chopped
- FOR THE CANADIAN BACON
- ¼ cup brewed coffee
- 2 tablespoons maple syrup

- 1 tablespoon light brown sugar
- 6 slices Canadian bacon

Directions:

1. To prep the egg cups: In a medium bowl, whisk together the eggs and cream until well combined with a uniform, light color. Stir in the salt, black pepper, roasted red peppers, and spinach until combined.
2. Divide the egg mixture among 6 silicone muffin cups.
3. To prep the Canadian bacon: In a small bowl, whisk together the coffee, maple syrup, and brown sugar.
4. Using a basting brush, brush the glaze onto both sides of each slice of bacon.
5. To cook the egg cups and Canadian bacon: Install a crisper plate in each of the two baskets. Place the egg cups in the Zone 1 basket and insert the basket in the unit. Place the glazed bacon in the Zone 2 basket, making sure the slices don't overlap, and insert the basket in the unit. It is okay if the bacon overlaps a little bit.
6. Select Zone 1, select BAKE, set the temperature to 325°F, and set the time to 13 minutes.
7. Select Zone 2, select AIR FRY, set the temperature to 400°F, and set the time to 5 minutes. Select SMART FINISH.
8. Press START/PAUSE to begin cooking.
9. When the Zone 2 timer reads 2 minutes, press START/PAUSE. Remove the basket and use silicone-tipped tongs to flip the bacon. Reinsert the basket and press START/PAUSE to resume cooking.
10. When cooking is complete, serve the egg cups with the Canadian bacon.

Nutrition Info:

- (Per serving) Calories: 180; Total fat: 9.5g; Saturated fat: 4.5g; Carbohydrates: 9g; Fiber: 0g; Protein: 14g; Sodium: 688mg

Quiche Breakfast Peppers

Servings: 4
Cooking Time: 15 Minutes
Ingredients:

- 4 eggs
- ½ tsp garlic powder
- 112g mozzarella cheese, shredded
- 125g ricotta cheese
- 2 bell peppers, cut in half & remove seeds
- 7½g baby spinach, chopped
- 22g parmesan cheese, grated
- ¼ tsp dried parsley

Directions:

1. In a bowl, whisk eggs, ricotta cheese, garlic powder, parsley, cheese, and spinach.
2. Pour the egg mixture into each bell pepper half and top with mozzarella cheese.

3. Insert a crisper plate in the Ninja Foodi air fryer baskets.

4. Place bell peppers in both the baskets.

5. Select zone 1 then select "air fry" mode and set the temperature to 355 degrees F for 15 minutes. Press "match" to match zone 2 settings to zone 1. Press "start/stop" to begin.

Nutrition Info:

- (Per serving) Calories 136 | Fat 7.6g |Sodium 125mg | Carbs 6.9g | Fiber 0.9g | Sugar 3.5g | Protein 10.8g

Banana And Raisins Muffins

Servings:2

Cooking Time:16

Ingredients:

- Salt, pinch
- 2 eggs, whisked
- 1/3 cup butter, melted
- 4 tablespoons of almond milk
- ¼ teaspoon of vanilla extract
- ½ teaspoon of baking powder
- 1-1/2 cup all-purpose flour
- 1 cup mashed bananas
- 2 tablespoons of raisins

Directions:

1. Take about 4 large (one-cup sized) ramekins and layer them with muffin papers.

2. Crack eggs in a large bowl, and whisk it all well and start adding vanilla extract, almond milk, baking powder, and melted butter

3. Whisk the ingredients very well.

4. Take a separate bowl and add the all-purpose flour, and salt.

5. Now, combine the add dry ingredients with the wet ingredients.

6. Now, pour mashed bananas and raisins into this batter

7. Mix it well to make a batter for the muffins.

8. Now pour the batter into four ramekins and divided the ramekins in the air fryer zones.

9. Set the timer for zone 1 to 16 minutes at 350 degrees F.

10. Select the MATCH button for the zone 2 basket.

11. Check if not done, and let it AIR FRY for one more minute.

12. Once it is done, serve.

Nutrition Info:

- (Per serving) Calories 727| Fat 43.1g| Sodium366 mg | Carbs 74.4g | Fiber 4.7g | Sugar 16.1g | Protein 14.1g

Sausage & Butternut Squash

Servings: 2

Cooking Time: 20 Minutes

Ingredients:

- 450g butternut squash, diced
- 70g kielbasa, diced
- ¼ onion, diced
- ¼ tsp garlic powder
- ½ tbsp olive oil
- Pepper
- Salt

Directions:

1. In a bowl, toss butternut squash with garlic powder, oil, onion, kielbasa, pepper, and salt.

2. Insert a crisper plate in the Ninja Foodi air fryer baskets.

3. Add sausage and butternut squash mixture in both baskets.

4. Select zone 1, then select "air fry" mode and set the temperature to 375 degrees F for 20 minutes. Press "match" to match zone 2 settings to zone 1. Press "start/stop" to begin. Stir halfway through.

Nutrition Info:

- (Per serving) Calories 68 | Fat 3.6g |Sodium 81mg | Carbs 9.7g | Fiber 1.7g | Sugar 2.2g | Protein 0.9g

Sweet Potato Hash

Servings: 4

Cooking Time: 15 Minutes

Ingredients:

- 3 sweet potatoes, peel & cut into ½-inch pieces
- ½ tsp cinnamon
- 2 tbsp olive oil
- 1 bell pepper, cut into ½-inch pieces
- ½ tsp dried thyme
- ½ tsp nutmeg
- 1 medium onion, cut into ½-inch pieces
- Pepper
- Salt

Directions:

1. In a bowl, toss sweet potatoes with the remaining ingredients.

2. Insert a crisper plate in Ninja Foodi air fryer baskets.

3. Add potato mixture in both baskets.

4. Select zone 1 then select "air fry" mode and set the temperature to 355 degrees F for 15 minutes. Press "match" to match zone 2 settings to zone 1. Press "start/stop" to begin.

Nutrition Info:

- (Per serving) Calories 167 | Fat 7.3g |Sodium 94mg | Carbs 24.9g | Fiber 4.2g | Sugar 6.8g | Protein 2.2g

Brussels Sprouts Potato Hash

Servings: 4

Cooking Time: 10 Minutes

Ingredients:

- 455g Brussels sprouts
- 1 small to medium red onion
- 227g baby red potatoes
- 2 tablespoons avocado oil
- ½ teaspoon salt
- ½ teaspoon black pepper

Directions:

1. Peel and boil potatoes in salted water for 15 minutes until soft.
2. Drain and allow them to cool down then dice.
3. Shred Brussels sprouts and toss them with potatoes and the rest of the ingredients.
4. Divide this veggies hash mixture in both of the air fryer baskets.
5. Return the air fryer basket 1 to Zone 1, and basket 2 to Zone 2 of the Ninja Foodi 2-Basket Air Fryer.
6. Choose the "Air Fry" mode for Zone 1 with 375 degrees F temperature and 10 minutes of cooking time.
7. Select the "MATCH COOK" option to copy the settings for Zone 2.
8. Initiate cooking by pressing the START/PAUSE BUTTON.
9. Shake the veggies once cooked halfway through.
10. Serve warm.

Nutrition Info:

- (Per serving) Calories 305 | Fat 25g |Sodium 532mg | Carbs 2.3g | Fiber 0.4g | Sugar 2g | Protein 18.3g

Egg With Baby Spinach

Servings:4

Cooking Time:12

Ingredients:

- Nonstick spray, for greasing ramekins
- 2 tablespoons olive oil
- 6 ounces baby spinach
- 2 garlic cloves, minced
- 1/3 teaspoon kosher salt
- 6-8 large eggs
- ½ cup half and half
- Salt and black pepper, to taste
- 8 Sourdough bread slices, toasted

Directions:

1. Grease 4 ramekins with oil spray and set aside for further use.
2. Take a skillet and heat oil in it.

3. Then cook spinach for 2 minutes and add garlic and salt black pepper.
4. Let it simmer for2more minutes.
5. Once the spinach is wilted, transfer it to a plate.
6. Whisk an egg into a small bowl.
7. Add in the spinach.
8. Whisk it well and then pour half and half.
9. Divide this mixture between 4 ramekins and remember not to overfill it to the top, leave a little space on top.
10. Put the ramekins in zone 1 and zone 2 baskets of the Ninja Foodie 2-Basket Air Fryer.
11. Press start and set zone 1 to AIR fry it at 350 degrees F for 8-12 minutes.
12. Press the MATCH button for zone 2.
13. Once it's cooked and eggs are done, serve with sourdough bread slices.

Nutrition Info:

- (Per serving) Calories 404| Fat 19.6g| Sodium 761mg | Carbs 40.1g | Fiber 2.5g| Sugar 2.5g | Protein 19.2g

Sausage Hash And Baked Eggs

Servings:4

Cooking Time: 30 Minutes

Ingredients:

- FOR THE HASH
- 2 yellow potatoes (about 1 pound), cut into ½-inch pieces
- 4 garlic cloves, minced
- 1 teaspoon kosher salt
- ¼ teaspoon freshly ground black pepper
- 2 tablespoons olive oil
- ½ pound pork breakfast sausage meat
- 1 small yellow onion, diced
- 1 red bell pepper, diced
- 1 teaspoon Italian seasoning
- FOR THE EGGS
- Nonstick cooking spray
- 4 large eggs
- 4 tablespoons water

Directions:

1. To prep the hash: In a large bowl, combine the potatoes, garlic, salt, black pepper, and olive oil and toss to coat. Crumble in the sausage and mix until combined.
2. To prep the eggs: Mist 4 silicone muffin cups with cooking spray. Crack 1 egg into each muffin cup. Top each egg with 1 tablespoon of water.
3. To cook the hash and eggs: Install a crisper plate in the Zone 1 basket. Place the sausage and potato mixture in the Zone 1 basket and insert the basket in the unit. Place the egg cups in the Zone 2 basket and insert the basket in the unit.
4. Select Zone 1, select AIR FRY, set the temperature to 400°F, and set the time to 30 minutes.

5. Select Zone 2, select BAKE, set the temperature to 325°F, and set the time to 12 minutes. Select SMART FINISH.

6. Press START/PAUSE to begin cooking.

7. When the Zone 1 timer reads 20 minutes, press START/PAUSE. Remove the basket and add the onion, bell pepper, and Italian seasoning to the hash. Mix until combined, breaking up any large pieces of sausage. Reinsert the basket and press START/PAUSE to resume cooking.

8. When cooking is complete, serve the hash topped with an egg.

Nutrition Info:

- (Per serving) Calories: 400; Total fat: 23g; Saturated fat: 5.5g; Carbohydrates: 31g; Fiber: 2g; Protein: 19g; Sodium: 750mg

Morning Egg Rolls

Servings: 6
Cooking Time: 13 Minutes.

Ingredients:

- 2 eggs
- 2 tablespoons milk
- Salt, to taste
- Black pepper, to taste
- ½ cup shredded cheddar cheese
- 2 sausage patties
- 6 egg roll wrappers
- 1 tablespoon olive oil
- 1 cup water

Directions:

1. Grease a small skillet with some olive oil and place it over medium heat.

2. Add sausage patties and cook them until brown.

3. Chop the cooked patties into small pieces. Beat eggs with salt, black pepper, and milk in a mixing bowl.

4. Grease the same skillet with 1 teaspoon of olive oil and pour the egg mixture into it.

5. Stir cook to make scrambled eggs.

6. Add sausage, mix well and remove the skillet from the heat.

7. Spread an egg roll wrapper on the working surface in a diamond shape position.

8. Add a tablespoon of cheese at the bottom third of the roll wrapper.

9. Top the cheese with egg mixture and wet the edges of the wrapper with water.

10. Fold the two corners of the wrapper and roll it, then seal the edges.

11. Repeat the same steps and divide the rolls in the two crisper plates.

12. Return the crisper plates to the Ninja Foodi Dual Zone Air Fryer.

13. Choose the Air Fry mode for Zone 1 and set the temperature to 375 degrees F and the time to 13 minutes.

14. Select the "MATCH" button to copy the settings for Zone 2.

15. Initiate cooking by pressing the START/STOP button.

16. Flip the rolls after 8 minutes and continue cooking for another 5 minutes.

17. Serve warm and fresh.

Nutrition Info:

- (Per serving) Calories 282 | Fat 15g |Sodium 526mg | Carbs 20g | Fiber 0.6g | Sugar 3.3g | Protein 16g

Breakfast Cheese Sandwich

Servings: 2
Cooking Time: 8 Minutes
Ingredients:

- 4 bread slices
- 2 provolone cheese slice
- ¼ tsp dried basil
- 2 tbsp mayonnaise
- 2 Monterey jack cheese slice
- 2 cheddar cheese slice
- ¼ tsp dried oregano

Directions:

1. In a small bowl, mix mayonnaise, basil, and oregano.

2. Spread mayonnaise on one side of the two bread slices.

3. Top two bread slices with cheddar cheese, provolone cheese, Monterey jack cheese slice, and cover with remaining bread slices.

4. Insert a crisper plate in the Ninja Foodi air fryer baskets.

5. Place sandwiches in both baskets.

6. Select zone 1, then select "air fry" mode and set the temperature to 390 degrees F for 8 minutes. Press "match" to match zone 2 settings to zone 1. Press "start/stop" to begin. Turn halfway through.

Nutrition Info:

- (Per serving) Calories 421 | Fat 30.7g |Sodium 796mg | Carbs 13.9g | Fiber 0.5g | Sugar 2.2g | Protein 22.5g

Air Fryer Sausage Patties

Servings: 12

Cooking Time: 10 Minutes

Ingredients:

- 1-pound pork sausage or ready-made patties
- Fennel seeds or preferred seasonings

Directions:

1. Prepare the sausage by slicing it into patties, then flavor it with fennel seed or your favorite seasonings.

2. Install a crisper plate in both drawers. Place half the patties in zone 1 and half in zone 2, then insert the drawers into the unit.

3. Select zone 1, select AIR FRY, set temperature to 390 degrees F/ 200 degrees C, and set time to 10 minutes.

4. Select MATCH to match zone 2 settings to zone 1.

5. Press the START/STOP button to begin cooking.

6. When cooking is complete, remove the patties from the unit and serve with sauce or make a burger.

Nutrition Info:

- (Per serving) Calories 130 | Fat 10.5g | Sodium 284mg | Carbs 0.3g | Fiber 0.2g | Sugar 0g | Protein 7.4g

Bagels

Servings: 8

Cooking Time: 15 Minutes

Ingredients:

- 2 cups self-rising flour
- 2 cups non-fat plain Greek yogurt
- 2 beaten eggs for egg wash (optional)
- ½ cup sesame seeds (optional)

Directions:

1. In a medium mixing bowl, combine the self-rising flour and Greek yogurt using a wooden spoon.

2. Knead the dough for about 5 minutes on a lightly floured board.

3. Divide the dough into four equal pieces and roll each into a thin rope, securing the ends to form a bagel shape.

4. Install a crisper plate in both drawers. Place 4 bagels in a single layer in each drawer. Insert the drawers into the unit.

5. Select zone 1, select AIR FRY, set temperature to 360 degrees F/ 180 degrees C, and set time to 15 minutes. Select MATCH to match zone 2 settings to zone 1. Select START/STOP to begin.

6. Once the timer has finished, remove the bagels from the units.

7. Serve and enjoy!

Nutrition Info:

- (Per serving) Calories 202 | Fat 4.5g | Sodium 55mg | Carbs 31.3g | Fiber 2.7g | Sugar 4.7g | Protein 8.7g

Snacks And Appetizers Recipes

Crispy Plantain Chips

Servings: 4
Cooking Time: 20 Minutes.
Ingredients:
- 1 green plantain
- 1 teaspoon canola oil
- ½ teaspoon sea salt

Directions:
1. Peel and cut the plantains into long strips using a mandolin slicer.
2. Grease the crisper plates with ½ teaspoon of canola oil.
3. Toss the plantains with salt and remaining canola oil.
4. Divide these plantains in the two crisper plates.
5. Return the crisper plate to the Ninja Foodi Dual Zone Air Fryer.
6. Choose the Air Fry mode for Zone 1 and set the temperature to 350 degrees F and the time to 20 minutes.
7. Select the "MATCH" button to copy the settings for Zone 2.
8. Initiate cooking by pressing the START/STOP button.
9. Toss the plantains after 10 minutes and resume cooking.
10. Serve warm.

Nutrition Info:
- (Per serving) Calories 122 | Fat 1.8g |Sodium 794mg | Carbs 17g | Fiber 8.9g | Sugar 1.6g | Protein 14.9g

Peppered Asparagus

Servings: 6
Cooking Time: 16 Minutes.
Ingredients:
- 1 bunch of asparagus, trimmed
- Avocado or Olive Oil
- Himalayan salt, to taste
- Black pepper, to taste

Directions:
1. Divide the asparagus in the two crisper plate.
2. Toss the asparagus with salt, black pepper, and oil.
3. Return the crisper plate to the Ninja Foodi Dual Zone Air Fryer.
4. Choose the Air Fry mode for Zone 1 and set the temperature to 390 degrees F and the time to 16 minutes.
5. Select the "MATCH" button to copy the settings for Zone 2.
6. Initiate cooking by pressing the START/STOP button.
7. Serve warm.

Nutrition Info:
- (Per serving) Calories 163 | Fat 11.5g |Sodium 918mg | Carbs 8.3g | Fiber 4.2g | Sugar 0.2g | Protein 7.4g

Roasted Tomato Bruschetta With Toasty Garlic Bread

Servings:4
Cooking Time: 12 Minutes
Ingredients:
- FOR THE ROASTED TOMATOES
- 10 ounces cherry tomatoes, cut in half
- 1 tablespoon balsamic vinegar
- 1 tablespoon olive oil
- ¼ teaspoon kosher salt
- ¼ teaspoon freshly ground black pepper
- FOR THE GARLIC BREAD
- 4 slices crusty Italian bread
- 1 tablespoon olive oil
- 3 garlic cloves, minced
- ¼ teaspoon Italian seasoning
- FOR THE BRUSCHETTA
- ¼ cup loosely packed fresh basil, thinly sliced
- ½ cup part-skim ricotta cheese

Directions:
1. To prep the tomatoes: In a small bowl, combine the tomatoes, vinegar, oil, salt, and black pepper.
2. To prep the garlic bread: Brush one side of each bread slice with the oil. Sprinkle with the garlic and Italian seasoning.
3. To cook the tomatoes and garlic bread: Install a broil rack in the Zone 1 basket (without the crisper plate installed). Place the tomatoes on the rack in the basket and insert the basket in the unit.
4. Place 2 slices of bread in the Zone 2 basket and insert the basket in the unit.
5. Select Zone 1, select AIR BROIL, set the temperature to 450°F, and set the time to 12 minutes.
6. Select Zone 2, select AIR FRY, set the temperature to 360°F, and set the time to 10 minutes. Select SMART FINISH.
7. Press START/PAUSE to begin cooking.
8. When the Zone 2 timer reads 5 minutes, press START/PAUSE. Remove the basket and transfer the garlic bread to a cutting board. Place the remaining 2 slices of garlic bread in the basket. Reinsert the basket in the unit and press START/PAUSE to resume cooking.
9. To assemble the bruschetta: When cooking is complete, add the basil to the tomatoes and stir to combine. Spread 2 tablespoons of ricotta onto each slice of garlic bread and top with the tomatoes. Serve warm or at room temperature.

Nutrition Info:

- (Per serving) Calories: 212; Total fat: 11g; Saturated fat: 2.5g; Carbohydrates: 22g; Fiber: 1.5g; Protein: 6g; Sodium: 286mg

Chicken Tenders

Servings:3
Cooking Time:12

Ingredients:

- 1 pound of chicken tender
- Salt and black pepper, to taste
- 1 cup Panko bread crumbs
- 2 cups Italian bread crumbs
- 1 cup parmesan cheese
- 2 eggs
- Oil spray, for greasing

Directions:

1. Sprinkle the tenders with salt and black pepper.
2. In a medium bowl mix Panko bread crumbs with Italian breadcrumbs.
3. Add salt, pepper, and parmesan cheese.
4. Crack two eggs in a bowl.
5. First, put the chicken tender in eggs.
6. Now dredge the tender in a bowl and coat the tender well with crumbs.
7. Line both of the baskets of the air fryer with parchment paper.
8. At the end spray the tenders with oil spray.
9. Divided the tenders between the baskets of Ninja Foodie 2-Basket Air Fryer.
10. Set zone 1 basket to AIR FRY mode at 350 degrees F for 12 minutes.
11. Select the MATCH button for the zone 2 basket.
12. Once it's done, serve.

Nutrition Info:

- (Per serving) Calories558 | Fat23.8g | Sodium872 mg | Carbs 20.9g | Fiber1.7 g| Sugar2.2 g | Protein 63.5g

Stuffed Mushrooms

Servings: 5
Cooking Time: 8 Minutes

Ingredients:

- 8 ounces fresh mushrooms (I used Monterey)
- 4 ounces cream cheese
- ¼ cup shredded parmesan cheese
- ⅛cup shredded sharp cheddar cheese
- ⅛ cup shredded white cheddar cheese
- 1 teaspoon Worcestershire sauce
- 2 garlic cloves, minced
- Salt and pepper, to taste

Directions:

1. To prepare the mushrooms for stuffing, remove their stems. Make a circle cut around the area where the stem used to be. Continue to cut until all of the superfluous mushroom is removed.
2. To soften the cream cheese, microwave it for 15 seconds.
3. Combine the cream cheese, shredded cheeses, salt, pepper, garlic, and Worcestershire sauce in a medium mixing bowl. To blend, stir everything together.
4. Stuff the mushrooms with the cheese mixture.
5. Place a crisper plate in each drawer. Put the stuffed mushrooms in a single layer in each drawer. Insert the drawers into the unit.
6. Select zone 1, then AIR FRY, then set the temperature to 360 degrees F/ 180 degrees C with an 8-minute timer. To match zone 2 settings to zone 1, choose MATCH. To begin, select START/STOP.
7. Serve and enjoy!

Nutrition Info:

- (Per serving) Calories 230 | Fat 9.5g | Sodium 105mg | Carbs 35.5g | Fiber 5.1g | Sugar 0.1g | Protein 7.1g

Garlic Bread

Servings: 4
Cooking Time: 10 Minutes

Ingredients:

- ½ loaf of bread
- 3 tablespoons butter, softened
- 3 garlic cloves, minced
- ½ teaspoon Italian seasoning
- Small pinch of red pepper flakes
- Optional
- ¼ cup shredded mozzarella cheese
- Freshly grated parmesan cheese
- Chopped fresh parsley for serving/topping

Directions:

1. Slice the bread in half horizontally or as appropriate to fit inside the air fryer.
2. Combine the softened butter, garlic, Italian seasoning, and red pepper flakes in a mixing bowl.
3. Brush the garlic butter mixture evenly over the bread.
4. Place a crisper plate in each drawer. Place the bread pieces into each drawer. Insert the drawers into the unit.
5. Select zone 1, then AIR FRY, then set the temperature to 360 degrees F/ 180 degrees C with a 6-minute timer. To match zone 2 settings to zone 1, choose MATCH. To begin, select START/STOP.
6. Remove the garlic bread from your air fryer, slice, and serve!

Nutrition Info:

- (Per serving) Calories 150 | Fat 8.2g | Sodium 208mg | Carbs 14.3g | Fiber 2.3g | Sugar 1.2g | Protein 4.9g

Crab Cakes

Servings: 4
Cooking Time: 10 Minutes
Ingredients:

- 227g lump crab meat
- 1 red capsicum, chopped
- 3 green onions, chopped
- 3 tablespoons mayonnaise
- 3 tablespoons breadcrumbs
- 2 teaspoons old bay seasoning
- 1 teaspoon lemon juice

Directions:

1. Mix crab meat with capsicum, onions and the rest of the ingredients in a food processor.
2. Make 4 inch crab cakes out of this mixture.
3. Divide the crab cakes into the Ninja Foodi 2 Baskets Air Fryer baskets.
4. Return the air fryer basket 1 to Zone 1, and basket 2 to Zone 2 of the Ninja Foodi 2-Basket Air Fryer.
5. Choose the "Air Fry" mode for Zone 1 at 370 degrees F and 10 minutes of cooking time.
6. Select the "MATCH COOK" option to copy the settings for Zone 2.
7. Initiate cooking by pressing the START/PAUSE BUTTON.
8. Flip the crab cakes once cooked halfway through.
9. Serve warm.

Nutrition Info:

- (Per serving) Calories 163 | Fat 11.5g |Sodium 918mg | Carbs 8.3g | Fiber 4.2g | Sugar 0.2g | Protein 7.4g

Stuffed Bell Peppers

Servings:3
Cooking Time:16
Ingredients:

- 6 large bell peppers
- 1-1/2 cup cooked rice
- 2 cups cheddar cheese

Directions:

1. Cut the bell peppers in half lengthwise and remove all the seeds.
2. Fill the cavity of each bell pepper with cooked rice.
3. Divide the bell peppers amongst the two zones of the air fryer basket.
4. Set the time for zone 1 for 200 degrees for 10 minutes.
5. Select MATCH button of zone 2 basket.
6. Afterward, take out the baskets and sprinkle cheese on top.
7. Set the time for zone 1 for 200 degrees for 6 minutes.
8. Select MATCH button of zone 2 basket.
9. Once it's done, serve.

Nutrition Info:

- (Per serving) Calories 605| Fat 26g | Sodium477 mg | Carbs68.3 g | Fiber4 g| Sugar 12.5g | Protein25.6 g

Parmesan French Fries

Servings: 6
Cooking Time: 20 Minutes.
Ingredients:

- 3 medium russet potatoes
- 2 tablespoons parmesan cheese
- 2 tablespoons fresh parsley, chopped
- 1 tablespoon olive oil
- Salt, to taste

Directions:

1. Wash the potatoes and pass them through the fries' cutter to get ¼-inch-thick fries.
2. Place the fries in a colander and drizzle salt on top.
3. Leave these fries for 10 minutes, then rinse.
4. Toss the potatoes with parmesan cheese, oil, salt, and parsley in a bowl.
5. Divide the potatoes into the two crisper plates.
6. Return the crisper plates to the Ninja Foodi Dual Zone Air Fryer.
7. Choose the Air Fry mode for Zone 1 and set the temperature to 360 degrees F and the time to 20 minutes.
8. Select the "MATCH" button to copy the settings for Zone 2.
9. Initiate cooking by pressing the START/STOP button.
10. Toss the chips once cooked halfway through, then resume cooking.
11. Serve warm.

Nutrition Info:

- (Per serving) Calories 307 | Fat 8.6g |Sodium 510mg | Carbs 22.2g | Fiber 1.4g | Sugar 13g | Protein 33.6g

Fried Pickles

Servings: 4
Cooking Time: 15 Minutes
Ingredients:

- 2 cups sliced dill pickles
- 1 cup flour
- 1 tablespoon garlic powder
- 1 tablespoon Cajun spice
- ½ tablespoon cayenne pepper
- Olive Oil or cooking spray

Directions:

1. Mix together the flour and spices in a bowl.
2. Coat the sliced pickles with the flour mixture.
3. Place a crisper plate in each drawer. Put the pickles in a single layer in each drawer. Insert the drawers into the unit.

4. Select zone 1, then AIR FRY, then set the temperature to 400 degrees F/ 200 degrees C with a 15-minute timer. To match zone 2 settings to zone 1, choose MATCH. To begin, select START/STOP.

Nutrition Info:
- (Per serving) Calories 161 | Fat 4.1g | Sodium 975mg | Carbs 27.5g | Fiber 2.2g | Sugar 1.5g | Protein 4g

Zucchini Chips

Servings: 4
Cooking Time: 15 Minutes
Ingredients:
- 1 medium-sized zucchini
- ½ cup panko breadcrumbs
- ½ teaspoon garlic powder
- ¼ teaspoon onion powder
- 1 egg
- 3 tablespoons flour

Directions:
1. Slice the zucchini into thin slices, about ¼-inch thick.
2. In a mixing bowl, combine the panko breadcrumbs, garlic powder, and onion powder.
3. The egg should be whisked in a different bowl, while the flour should be placed in a third bowl.
4. Dip the zucchini slices in the flour, then in the egg, and finally in the breadcrumbs.
5. Place a crisper plate in each drawer. Put the zucchini slices into each drawer in a single layer. Insert the drawers into the unit.
6. Select zone 1, then AIR FRY, then set the temperature to 360 degrees F/ 180 degrees C with a 6-minute timer. To match zone 2 settings to zone 1, choose MATCH. To begin, select START/STOP.
7. Remove the zucchini from the drawers after the timer has finished.

Nutrition Info:
- (Per serving) Calories 82 | Fat 1.5g | Sodium 89mg | Carbs 14.1g | Fiber 1.7g | Sugar 1.2g | Protein 3.9g

Miso-glazed Shishito Peppers Charred Lemon Shishito Peppers

Servings:4
Cooking Time: 10 Minutes
Ingredients:
- FOR THE MISO-GLAZED PEPPERS
- 2 tablespoons vegetable oil
- 2 tablespoons water
- 1 tablespoon white miso
- 1 teaspoon grated fresh ginger
- ½ pound shishito peppers

- FOR THE CHARRED LEMON PEPPERS
- ½ pound shishito peppers
- 1 lemon, cut into ⅛-inch-thick rounds
- 2 garlic cloves, minced
- 2 tablespoons vegetable oil
- ½ teaspoon kosher salt

Directions:
1. To prep the miso-glazed peppers: In a large bowl, mix the vegetable oil, water, miso, and ginger until well combined. Add the shishitos and toss to coat.
2. To prep the charred lemon peppers: In a large bowl, combine the shishitos, lemon slices, garlic, vegetable oil, and salt. Toss to coat.
3. To cook the peppers: Install a crisper plate in each of the two baskets. Place the miso-glazed peppers in the Zone 1 basket and insert the basket in the unit. Place the peppers with lemons in the Zone 2 basket and insert the basket in the unit.
4. Select Zone 1, select AIR FRY, set the temperature to 390°F, and set the time to 10 minutes. Select MATCH COOK to match Zone 2 settings to Zone 1.
5. Press START/PAUSE to begin cooking.
6. When both timers read 4 minutes, press START/PAUSE. Remove both baskets and shake well. Reinsert the baskets and press START/PAUSE to resume cooking.
7. When cooking is complete, serve immediately.

Nutrition Info:
- (Per serving) Calories: 165; Total fat: 14g; Saturated fat: 2g; Carbohydrates: 9g; Fiber: 2g; Protein: 2g; Sodium: 334mg

Beef Jerky Pineapple Jerky

Servings:8
Cooking Time: 6 To 12 Hours
Ingredients:
- FOR THE BEEF JERKY
- ½ cup reduced-sodium soy sauce
- ¼ cup pineapple juice
- 1 tablespoon dark brown sugar
- 1 tablespoon Worcestershire sauce
- ½ teaspoon smoked paprika
- ¼ teaspoon freshly ground black pepper
- ¼ teaspoon red pepper flakes
- 1 pound beef bottom round, trimmed of excess fat, cut into ¼-inch-thick slices
- FOR THE PINEAPPLE JERKY
- 1 pound pineapple, cut into ⅛-inch-thick rounds, pat dry
- 1 teaspoon chili powder (optional)

Directions:
1. To prep the beef jerky: In a large zip-top bag, combine the soy sauce, pineapple juice, brown sugar, Worcestershire sauce, smoked paprika, black pepper, and red pepper flakes.

2. Add the beef slices, seal the bag, and toss to coat the meat in the marinade. Refrigerate overnight or for at least 8 hours.

3. Remove the beef slices and discard the marinade. Using a paper towel, pat the slices dry to remove excess marinade.

4. To prep the pineapple jerky: Sprinkle the pineapple with chili powder (if using).

5. To dehydrate the jerky: Arrange half of the beef slices in a single layer in the Zone 1 basket, making sure they do not overlap. Place a crisper plate on top of the beef slices and arrange the remaining slices in a single layer on top of the crisper plate. Insert the basket in the unit.

6. Repeat this process with the pineapple in the Zone 2 basket and insert the basket in the unit.

7. Select Zone 1, select DEHYDRATE, set the temperature to 150°F, and set the time to 8 hours.

8. Select Zone 2, select DEHYDRATE, set the temperature to 135°F, and set the time to 12 hours.

9. Press START/PAUSE to begin cooking.

10. When the Zone 1 timer reads 2 hours, press START/PAUSE. Remove the basket and check the beef jerky for doneness. If necessary, reinsert the basket and press START/PAUSE to resume cooking.

Nutrition Info:

- (Per serving) Calories: 171; Total fat: 6.5g; Saturated fat: 2g; Carbohydrates: 2g; Fiber: 0g; Protein: 25g; Sodium: 369mg

Mozzarella Balls

Servings: 6
Cooking Time: 13 Minutes
Ingredients:

- 2 cups mozzarella, shredded
- 3 tablespoons cornstarch
- 3 tablespoons water
- 2 eggs, beaten
- 1 cup Italian seasoned breadcrumbs
- 1 tablespoon Italian seasoning
- 1½ teaspoons garlic powder
- 1 teaspoon salt
- 1½ teaspoons Parmesan

Directions:

1. Mix mozzarella with parmesan, water and cornstarch in a bowl.

2. Make 1-inch balls out of this mixture.

3. Mix breadcrumbs with seasoning, salt, and garlic powder in a bowl.

4. Dip the balls into the beaten eggs and coat with the breadcrumbs.

5. Place the coated balls in the air fryer baskets.

6. Return the air fryer basket 1 to Zone 1, and basket 2 to Zone 2 of the Ninja Foodi 2-Basket Air Fryer.

7. Choose the "Air Fry" mode for Zone 1 and set the temperature to 360 degrees F and 13 minutes of cooking time.

8. Select the "MATCH COOK" option to copy the settings for Zone 2.

9. Initiate cooking by pressing the START/PAUSE BUTTON.

10. Toss the balls once cooked halfway through.

11. Serve.

Nutrition Info:

- (Per serving) Calories 307 | Fat 8.6g |Sodium 510mg | Carbs 22.2g | Fiber 1.4g | Sugar 13g | Protein 33.6g

Cheese Stuffed Mushrooms

Servings: 4
Cooking Time: 8 Minutes
Ingredients:

- 176g button mushrooms, clean & cut stems
- 46g sour cream
- 17g cream cheese, softened
- ½ tsp garlic powder
- 58g cheddar cheese, shredded
- Pepper
- Salt

Directions:

1. In a small bowl, mix cream cheese, garlic powder, sour cream, pepper, and salt.

2. Stuff cream cheese mixture into each mushroom and top each with cheddar cheese.

3. Insert a crisper plate in the Ninja Foodi air fryer baskets.

4. Place the stuffed mushrooms in both baskets.

5. Select zone 1 then select "air fry" mode and set the temperature to 370 degrees F for 8 minutes. Press "match" to match zone 2 settings to zone 1. Press "start/stop" to begin.

Nutrition Info:

- (Per serving) Calories 222 | Fat 19.4g |Sodium 220mg | Carbs 5.6g | Fiber 1.2g | Sugar 2.2g | Protein 8.9g

Potato Chips

Servings: 4
Cooking Time: 16 Minutes
Ingredients:

- 2 large potatoes, peeled and sliced
- 1½ teaspoons salt
- 1½ teaspoons black pepper
- Oil for misting

Directions:

1. Soak potatoes in cold water for 30 minutes then drain.

2. Pat dry the potato slices and toss them with cracked pepper, salt and oil mist.

3. Spread the potatoes in the air fryer basket.

4. Return the air fryer basket 1 to Zone 1, and basket 2 to Zone 2 of the Ninja Foodi 2-Basket Air Fryer.

5. Choose the "Air Fry" mode for Zone 1 at 300 degrees F and 16 minutes of cooking time.

6. Select the "MATCH COOK" option to copy the settings for Zone 2.

7. Initiate cooking by pressing the START/PAUSE BUTTON.

8. Toss the fries once cooked halfway through.

9. Serve warm.

Nutrition Info:

- (Per serving) Calories 122 | Fat 1.8g |Sodium 794mg | Carbs 17g | Fiber 8.9g | Sugar 1.6g | Protein 14.9g

Cheese Corn Fritters

Servings: 6
Cooking Time: 12 Minutes
Ingredients:

- 1 egg
- 164g corn
- 2 green onions, diced
- 45g flour
- 29g breadcrumbs
- 117g cheddar cheese, shredded
- ½ tsp onion powder
- ½ tsp garlic powder
- 15g sour cream
- Pepper
- Salt

Directions:

1. In a large bowl, add all ingredients and mix until well combined.

2. Insert a crisper plate in the Ninja Foodi air fryer baskets.

3. Make patties from the mixture and place them in both baskets.

4. Select zone 1, then select "air fry" mode and set the temperature to 370 degrees F for 12 minutes. Press "match" to match zone 2 settings to zone 1. Press "start/stop" to begin. Turn halfway through.

Nutrition Info:

- (Per serving) Calories 100 | Fat 4.8g |Sodium 135mg | Carbs 10g | Fiber 1.1g | Sugar 1.5g | Protein 5g

Mac And Cheese Balls

Servings: 4
Cooking Time: 20 Minutes
Ingredients:

- 1 cup panko breadcrumbs
- 4 cups prepared macaroni and cheese, refrigerated
- 3 tablespoons flour
- 1 teaspoon salt, divided

- 1 teaspoon ground black pepper, divided
- 1 teaspoon smoked paprika, divided
- ½ teaspoon garlic powder, divided
- 2 eggs
- 1 tablespoon milk
- ¼ cup ranch dressing, garlic aioli, or chipotle mayo, for dipping (optional)

Directions:

1. Preheat a conventional oven to 400 degrees F/ 200 degrees C.

2. Shake the breadcrumbs onto a baking sheet so that they're evenly distributed. Bake in the oven for 3 minutes, then shake and bake for an additional 1 to 2 minutes, or until toasted.

3. Form the chilled macaroni and cheese into golf ball-sized balls and set them aside.

4. Combine the flour, ½ teaspoon salt, ½ teaspoon black pepper, ½ teaspoon smoked paprika, and ¼ teaspoon garlic powder in a large mixing bowl.

5. In a small bowl, whisk together the eggs and milk.

6. Combine the breadcrumbs, remaining salt, pepper, paprika, and garlic powder in a mixing bowl.

7. To coat the macaroni and cheese balls, roll them in the flour mixture, then the egg mixture, and then the breadcrumb mixture.

8. Place a crisper plate in each drawer. Put the cheese balls in a single layer in each drawer. Insert the drawers into the unit.

9. Select zone 1, then AIR FRY, then set the temperature to 360 degrees F/ 180 degrees C with an 8-minute timer. To match zone 2 settings to zone 1, choose MATCH. To begin, select START/STOP.

10. Serve and enjoy!

Nutrition Info:

- (Per serving) Calories 489 | Fat 15.9g | Sodium 1402mg | Carbs 69.7g | Fiber 2.5g | Sugar 4g | Protein 16.9g

Strawberries And Walnuts Muffins

Servings:2
Cooking Time:15
Ingredients:

- Salt, pinch
- 2 eggs, whisked
- 1/3 cup maple syrup
- 1/3 cup coconut oil
- 4 tablespoons of water
- 1 teaspoon of orange zest
- ¼ teaspoon of vanilla extract
- ½ teaspoon of baking powder
- 1 cup all-purpose flour
- 1 cup strawberries, finely chopped
- 1/3 cup walnuts, chopped and roasted

Directions:

1. Take one cup size of 4 ramekins that are oven safe.
2. Layer it with muffin paper.
3. In a bowl and add egg, maple syrup, oil, water, vanilla extract, and orange zest.
4. Whisk it all very well
5. In a separate bowl, mix flour, baking powder, and salt.
6. Now add dry ingredients slowly to wet ingredients.
7. Now pour this batter into ramekins and top it with strawberries and walnuts.
8. Now divide it between both zones and set the time for zone 1 basket to 15 minutes at 350 degrees F.
9. Select the MATCH button for the zone 2 basket.
10. Check if not done let it AIR FRY FOR one more minute.
11. Once done, serve.

Nutrition Info:

- (Per serving) Calories 897| Fat 53.9g | Sodium 148mg | Carbs 92g | Fiber 4.7g| Sugar35.6 g | Protein 17.5g

Crab Cake Poppers

Servings: 6
Cooking Time: 10 Minutes
Ingredients:

- 1 egg, lightly beaten
- 453g lump crab meat, drained
- 1 tsp garlic, minced
- 1 tsp lemon juice
- 1 tsp old bay seasoning
- 30g almond flour
- 1 tsp Dijon mustard
- 28g mayonnaise
- Pepper
- Salt

Directions:

1. In a bowl, mix crab meat and remaining ingredients until well combined.
2. Make small balls from the crab meat mixture and place them on a plate.
3. Place the plate in the refrigerator for 50 minutes.
4. Insert a crisper plate in the Ninja Foodi air fryer baskets.
5. Place the prepared crab meatballs in both baskets.
6. Select zone 1 then select "air fry" mode and set the temperature to 360 degrees F for 10 minutes. Press "match" to match zone 2 settings to zone 1. Press "start/stop" to begin.

Nutrition Info:

- (Per serving) Calories 86 | Fat 8.5g |Sodium 615mg | Carbs 2.7g | Fiber 0.1g | Sugar 0.4g | Protein 12g

Fried Cheese

Servings: 4
Cooking Time: 12 Minutes
Ingredients:

- 1 Mozzarella cheese block, cut into sticks
- 2 teaspoons olive oil

Directions:

1. Divide the cheese slices into the Ninja Foodi 2 Baskets Air Fryer baskets.
2. Drizzle olive oil over the cheese slices.
3. Return the air fryer basket 1 to Zone 1, and basket 2 to Zone 2 of the Ninja Foodi 2-Basket Air Fryer.
4. Choose the "Air Fry" mode for Zone 1 and set the temperature to 360 degrees F and 12 minutes of cooking time.
5. Flip the cheese slices once cooked halfway through.
6. Serve.

Nutrition Info:

- (Per serving) Calories 186 | Fat 3g |Sodium 223mg | Carbs 31g | Fiber 8.7g | Sugar 5.5g | Protein 9.7g

Avocado Fries With Sriracha Dip

Servings: 4
Cooking Time: 6 Minutes
Ingredients:

- Avocado Fries
- 4 avocados, peeled and cut into sticks
- ¾ cup panko breadcrumbs
- ¼ cup flour
- 2 eggs, beaten
- ½ teaspoon garlic powder
- ½ teaspoon salt
- SRIRACHA-RANCH SAUCE
- ¼ cup ranch dressing
- 1 teaspoon sriracha sauce

Directions:

1. Mix flour with garlic powder and salt in a bowl.
2. Dredge the avocado sticks through the flour mixture.
3. Dip them in the eggs and coat them with breadcrumbs.
4. Place the coated fries in the air fryer baskets.
5. Return the air fryer basket 1 to Zone 1, and basket 2 to Zone 2 of the Ninja Foodi 2-Basket Air Fryer.
6. Choose the "Air Fry" mode for Zone 1 at 400 degrees F and 6 minutes of cooking time.
7. Select the "MATCH COOK" option to copy the settings for Zone 2.
8. Initiate cooking by pressing the START/PAUSE BUTTON.
9. Flip the fries once cooked halfway through.
10. Mix all the dipping sauce ingredients in a bowl.
11. Serve the fries with dipping sauce.

Nutrition Info:

- (Per serving) Calories 229 | Fat 1.9 |Sodium 567mg | Carbs 1.9g | Fiber 0.4g | Sugar 0.6g | Protein 11.8g

Cheddar Quiche

Servings:2
Cooking Time:12
Ingredients:
- 4 eggs, organic
- 1-1/4 cup heavy cream
- Salt, pinch
- ½ cup broccoli florets
- ½ cup cheddar cheese, shredded and for sprinkling

Directions:
1. Take a Pyrex pitcher and crack two eggs in it.
2. And fill it with heavy cream, about half the way up.
3. Add in the salt and then add in the broccoli and pour this into two quiche dishes, and top it with shredded cheddar cheese.
4. Now divide it between both zones of baskets.
5. For zone 1, set the time to 10-12 minutes at 325 degrees F.
6. Select the MATCH button for the zone 2 basket.
7. Once done, serve hot.

Nutrition Info:
- (Per serving) Calories 454| Fat40g | Sodium 406mg | Carbs 4.2g | Fiber 0.6g| Sugar1.3 g | Protein 20g

Chili-lime Crispy Chickpeas Pizza-seasoned Crispy Chickpeas

Servings:6
Cooking Time: 20 Minutes
Ingredients:
- FOR THE CHILI-LIME CHICKPEAS
- 1½ cups canned chickpeas, rinsed and drained
- ¼ cup fresh lime juice
- 1 tablespoon olive oil
- 1½ teaspoons chili powder
- ½ teaspoon kosher salt
- FOR THE PIZZA-SEASONED CHICKPEAS
- 1½ cups canned chickpeas, rinsed and drained
- 1 tablespoon olive oil
- 1 tablespoon grated Parmesan cheese
- ½ teaspoon dried basil
- ½ teaspoon dried oregano
- ½ teaspoon kosher salt
- ¼ teaspoon onion powder
- ¼ teaspoon garlic powder
- ¼ teaspoon fennel seeds
- ¼ teaspoon dried thyme
- ¼ teaspoon red pepper flakes (optional)

Directions:
1. To prep the chili-lime chickpeas: In a small bowl, mix the chickpeas, lime juice, olive oil, chili powder, and salt until the chickpeas are well coated.

2. To prep the pizza-seasoned chickpeas: In a small bowl, mix the chickpeas, olive oil, Parmesan, basil, oregano, salt, onion powder, garlic powder, fennel, thyme, and red pepper flakes (if using) until the chickpeas are well coated.
3. To cook the chickpeas: Install a crisper plate in each of the two baskets. Place the chili-lime chickpeas in the Zone 1 basket and insert the basket in the unit. Place the pizza-seasoned chickpeas in the Zone 2 basket and insert the basket in the unit.
4. Select Zone 1, select AIR FRY, set the temperature to 375°F, and set the time to 20 minutes. Select MATCH COOK to match Zone 2 settings to Zone 1.
5. Press START/PAUSE to begin cooking.
6. When both timers read 10 minutes, press START/PAUSE. Remove both baskets and give each basket a shake to redistribute the chickpeas. Reinsert both baskets and press START/PAUSE to resume cooking.
7. When both timers read 5 minutes, press START/PAUSE. Remove both baskets and give each basket a good shake again. Reinsert both baskets and press START/PAUSE to resume cooking.
8. When cooking is complete, the chickpeas will be crisp and golden brown. Serve warm or at room temperature.

Nutrition Info:
- (Per serving) Calories: 145; Total fat: 6.5g; Saturated fat: 0.5g; Carbohydrates: 17g; Fiber: 4.5g; Protein: 5g; Sodium: 348mg

Tater Tots

Servings: 4
Cooking Time: 8 Minutes
Ingredients:
- 16 ounces tater tots
- ½ cup shredded cheddar cheese
- 1½ teaspoons bacon bits
- 2 green onions, chopped
- Sour cream (optional)

Directions:
1. Place a crisper plate in each drawer. Put the tater tots into the drawers in a single layer. Insert the drawers into the unit.
2. Select zone 1, then AIR FRY, then set the temperature to 360 degrees F/ 180 degrees C with a 6-minute timer. To match zone 2 settings to zone 1, choose MATCH. To begin, select START/STOP.
3. When the cooking time is over, add the shredded cheddar cheese, bacon bits, and green onions over the tater tots. Select zone 1, AIR FRY, 360 degrees F/ 180 degrees C, for 4 minutes. Select MATCH. Press START/STOP.
4. Drizzle sour cream over the top before serving.
5. Enjoy!

Nutrition Info:
- (Per serving) Calories 335 | Fat 19.1g | Sodium 761mg | Carbs 34.1g | Fiber 3g | Sugar 0.6g | Protein 8.9g

Poultry Recipes

Yummy Chicken Breasts

Servings:2

Cooking Time:25

Ingredients:

- 4 large chicken breasts, 6 ounces each
- 2 tablespoons of oil bay seasoning
- 1 tablespoon Montreal chicken seasoning
- 1 teaspoon of thyme
- 1/2 teaspoon of paprika
- Salt, to taste
- oil spray, for greasing

Directions:

1. Season the chicken breast pieces with the listed seasoning and let them rest for 40 minutes.
2. Grease both sides of the chicken breast pieces with oil spray.
3. Divide the chicken breast piece between both baskets.
4. Set zone 1 to AIRFRY mode at 400 degrees F, for 15 minutes.
5. Select the MATCH button for another basket.
6. Select pause and take out the baskets and flip the chicken breast pieces, after 15 minutes.
7. Select the zones to 400 degrees F for 10 more minutes using the MATCH cook button.
8. Once it's done serve.

Nutrition Info:

- (Per serving) Calories 711| Fat 27.7g| Sodium 895mg | Carbs 1.6g | Fiber 0.4g | Sugar 0.1g | Protein 106.3g

Glazed Thighs With French Fries

Servings:3

Cooking Time:35

Ingredients:

- 2 tablespoons of Soy Sauce
- Salt, to taste
- 1 teaspoon of Worcestershire Sauce
- 2 teaspoons Brown Sugar
- 1 teaspoon of Ginger, paste
- 1 teaspoon of Garlic, paste
- 6 Boneless Chicken Thighs
- 1 pound of hand-cut potato fries
- 2 tablespoons of canola oil

Directions:

1. Coat the French fries well with canola oil.
2. Season it with salt.
3. In a small bowl, combine the soy sauce, Worcestershire sauce, brown sugar, ginger, and garlic.

4. Place the chicken in this marinade and let it sit for 40 minutes.
5. Put the chicken thighs into the zone 1 basket and fries into the zone 2 basket.
6. Press button 1 for the first basket, and set it to ROAST mode at 350 degrees F for 35 minutes.
7. For the second basket hit 2 and set time to 30 minutes at 360 degrees F, by selecting AIR FRY mode.
8. Once the cooking cycle completely take out the fries and chicken and serve it hot.

Nutrition Info:

- (Per serving) Calories 858| Fat39g | Sodium 1509mg | Carbs 45.6g | Fiber 4.4g | Sugar3 g | Protein 90g

Chicken Leg Piece

Servings:1

Cooking Time:25

Ingredients:

- 1 teaspoon of onion powder
- 1 teaspoon of paprika powder
- 1 teaspoon of garlic powder
- Salt and black pepper, to taste
- 1 tablespoon of Italian seasoning
- 1 teaspoon of celery seeds
- 2 eggs, whisked
- 1/3 cup buttermilk
- 1 cup of corn flour
- 1 pound of chicken leg

Directions:

1. Take a bowl and whisk egg along with pepper, salt, and buttermilk.
2. Set it aside for further use.
3. Mix all the spices in a small separate bowl.
4. Dredge the chicken in egg wash then dredge it in seasoning.
5. Coat the chicken legs with oil spray.
6. At the end dust it with the corn flour.
7. Divide the leg pieces into two zones.
8. Set zone 1 basket to 400 degrees F, for 25 minutes.
9. Select MATCH for zone 2 basket.
10. Let the air fryer do the magic.
11. Once it's done, serve and enjoy.

Nutrition Info:

- (Per serving) Calories 1511| Fat 52.3g| Sodium615 mg | Carbs 100g | Fiber 9.2g | Sugar 8.1g | Protein 154.2g

General Tso's Chicken

Servings: 4

Cooking Time: 22 Minutes.

Ingredients:

- 1 egg, large
- ⅓ cup 2 teaspoons cornstarch,
- ¼ teaspoons salt
- ¼ teaspoons ground white pepper
- 7 tablespoons chicken broth
- 2 tablespoons soy sauce
- 2 tablespoons ketchup
- 2 teaspoons sugar
- 2 teaspoons unseasoned rice vinegar
- 1 ½ tablespoons canola oil
- 4 chile de árbol, chopped and seeds discarded
- 1 tablespoon chopped fresh ginger
- 1 tablespoon garlic, chopped
- 2 tablespoons green onion, sliced
- 1 teaspoon toasted sesame oil
- 1 lb. boneless chicken thighs, cut into 1 ¼ -inch chunks
- ½ teaspoon toasted sesame seeds

Directions:

1. Add egg to a large bowl and beat it with a fork.
2. Add chicken to the egg and coat it well.
3. Whisk ⅓ cup of cornstarch with black pepper and salt in a small bowl.
4. Add chicken to the cornstarch mixture and mix well to coat.
5. Divide the chicken in the two crisper plates and spray them cooking oi.
6. Return the crisper plates to the Ninja Foodi Dual Zone Air Fryer.
7. Choose the Air Fry mode for Zone 1 and set the temperature to 390 degrees F and the time to 20 minutes.
8. Select the "MATCH" button to copy the settings for Zone 2.
9. Initiate cooking by pressing the START/STOP button.
10. Once done, remove the air fried chicken from the air fryer.
11. Whisk 2 teaspoons of cornstarch with soy sauce, broth, sugar, ketchup, and rice vinegar in a small bowl.
12. Add chilies and canola oil to a skillet and sauté for 1 minute.
13. Add garlic and ginger, then sauté for 30 seconds.
14. Stir in cornstarch sauce and cook until it bubbles and thickens.
15. Toss in cooked chicken and garnish with sesame oil, sesame seeds, and green onion.
16. Enjoy.

Nutrition Info:

- (Per serving) Calories 351 | Fat 16g |Sodium 777mg | Carbs 26g | Fiber 4g | Sugar 5g | Protein 28g

Crispy Sesame Chicken

Servings: 2

Cooking Time: 10 Minutes

Ingredients:

- 680g boneless chicken thighs, diced
- 2 tablespoons rice vinegar
- 1 tablespoon soy sauce
- 2 teaspoons minced fresh ginger
- 1 garlic clove, minced
- ¾ teaspoon salt
- ½ teaspoon black pepper
- 2 large eggs, beaten
- 1 cup cornstarch
- Sauce
- 59ml soy sauce
- 2 tablespoons rice vinegar
- ⅓ cup brown sugar
- 59ml water
- 1 tablespoon cornstarch
- 2 teaspoons sesame oil
- 2 tablespoons vegetable oil
- 2 garlic cloves, minced
- 2 teaspoons chile paste
- Garnish
- 1 tablespoon toasted sesame seeds

Directions:

1. Blend all the sauce ingredients in a saucepan and cook until it thickens then allow it to cool.
2. Mix chicken with black pepper, salt, garlic, ginger, vinegar, and soy sauce in a bowl.
3. Cover and marinate the chicken for 20 minutes.
4. Divide the chicken in the air fryer baskets.
5. Return the air fryer basket 1 to Zone 1, and basket 2 to Zone 2 of the Ninja Foodi 2-Basket Air Fryer.
6. Choose the "Air Fry" mode for Zone 1 and set the temperature to 400 degrees F and 10 minutes of cooking time.
7. Select the "MATCH COOK" option to copy the settings for Zone 2.
8. Initiate cooking by pressing the START/PAUSE BUTTON.
9. Pour the prepared sauce over the air fried chicken and drizzle sesame seeds on top.
10. Serve warm.

Nutrition Info:

- (Per serving) Calories 351 | Fat 16g |Sodium 777mg | Carbs 26g | Fiber 4g | Sugar 5g | Protein 28g

"fried" Chicken With Warm Baked Potato Salad

Servings:4
Cooking Time: 40 Minutes
Ingredients:

- FOR THE "FRIED" CHICKEN
- 1 cup buttermilk
- 1 tablespoon kosher salt
- 4 bone-in, skin-on chicken drumsticks and/or thighs
- 2 cups all-purpose flour
- 1 tablespoon seasoned salt
- 1 tablespoon paprika
- Nonstick cooking spray
- FOR THE POTATO SALAD
- 1½ pounds baby red potatoes, halved
- 1 tablespoon vegetable oil
- ½ cup mayonnaise
- ⅓ cup plain reduced-fat Greek yogurt
- 1 tablespoon apple cider vinegar
- ½ teaspoon kosher salt
- ½ teaspoon freshly ground black pepper
- ¾ cup shredded Cheddar cheese
- 4 slices cooked bacon, crumbled
- 3 scallions, sliced

Directions:

1. To prep the chicken: In a large bowl, combine the buttermilk and salt. Add the chicken and turn to coat. Let rest for at least 30 minutes (for the best flavor, marinate the chicken overnight in the refrigerator).

2. In a separate large bowl, combine the flour, seasoned salt, and paprika.

3. Remove the chicken from the marinade and allow any excess marinade to drip off. Discard the marinade. Dip the chicken pieces in the flour, coating them thoroughly. Mist with cooking spray. Let the chicken rest for 10 minutes.

4. To prep the potatoes: In a large bowl, combine the potatoes and oil and toss to coat.

5. To cook the chicken and potatoes: Install a crisper plate in the Zone 1 basket. Place the chicken in the basket in a single layer and insert the basket in the unit. Place the potatoes in the Zone 2 basket and insert the basket in the unit.

6. Select Zone 1, select AIR FRY, set the temperature to 390°F, and set the time to 30 minutes.

7. Select Zone 2, select BAKE, set the temperature to 400°F, and set the time to 40 minutes. Select SMART FINISH.

8. Press START/PAUSE to begin cooking.

9. When cooking is complete, the chicken will be golden brown and cooked through (an instant-read thermometer should read 165°F) and the potatoes will be fork-tender.

10. Rinse the potatoes under cold water for about 1 minute to cool them.

11. Place the potatoes in a large bowl and stir in the mayonnaise, yogurt, vinegar, salt, and black pepper. Gently stir in the Cheddar, bacon, and scallions. Serve warm with the "fried" chicken.

Nutrition Info:

- (Per serving) Calories: 639; Total fat: 38g; Saturated fat: 9.5g; Carbohydrates: 54g; Fiber: 4g; Protein: 21g; Sodium: 1,471mg

Chicken & Broccoli

Servings: 4
Cooking Time: 20 Minutes
Ingredients:

- 450g chicken breasts, boneless & cut into 1-inch pieces
- 1 tsp sesame oil
- 15ml soy sauce
- 1 tsp garlic powder
- 45ml olive oil
- 350g broccoli florets
- 2 tsp hot sauce
- 2 tsp rice vinegar
- Pepper
- Salt

Directions:

1. In a bowl, add chicken, broccoli florets, and remaining ingredients and mix well.

2. Insert a crisper plate in the Ninja Foodi air fryer baskets.

3. Add the chicken and broccoli mixture in both baskets.

4. Select zone 1, then select "air fry" mode and set the temperature to 380 degrees F for 20 minutes. Press "match" and press"start/stop" to begin.

Nutrition Info:

- (Per serving) Calories 337 | Fat 20.2g |Sodium 440mg | Carbs 3.9g | Fiber 1.3g | Sugar 1g | Protein 34.5g

Whole Chicken

Servings: 8
Cooking Time: 20 Minutes
Ingredients:

- 1 whole chicken (about 2.8 pounds), cut in half
- 4 tablespoons olive oil
- 2 teaspoons paprika
- 1 teaspoon garlic powder
- 1 teaspoon onion powder
- Salt and pepper, to taste

Directions:

1. Mix the olive oil, paprika, garlic powder, and onion powder together in a bowl.
2. Place the chicken halves, breast side up, on a plate. Spread a teaspoon or two of the oil mix all over the halves using either your hands or a brush. Season with salt and pepper.
3. Flip the chicken halves over and repeat on the other side. You'll want to reserve a little of the oil mix for later, but other than that, use it liberally.
4. Install a crisper plate in both drawers. Place one half of the chicken in the zone 1 drawer and the other half in the zone 2 drawer, then insert the drawers into the unit.
5. Select zone 1, select AIR FRY, set temperature to 390 degrees F/ 200 degrees C, and set time to 20 minutes. Select MATCH to match zone 2 settings to zone 1. Press the START/STOP button to begin cooking.
6. When cooking is done, check the internal temperature of the chicken. It should read 165°F. If the chicken isn't done, add more cooking time.

Nutrition Info:

- (Per serving) Calories 131 | Fat 8g | Sodium 51mg | Carbs 0g | Fiber 0g | Sugar 0g | Protein 14g

Cheddar-stuffed Chicken

Servings: 4
Cooking Time: 20 Minutes.
Ingredients:

- 3 bacon strips, cooked and crumbled
- 2 ounces Cheddar cheese, cubed
- ¼ cup barbeque sauce
- 2 (4 ounces) boneless chicken breasts
- Salt and black pepper to taste

Directions:

1. Make a 1-inch deep pouch in each chicken breast.
2. Mix cheddar cubes with half of the BBQ sauce, salt, black pepper, and bacon.
3. Divide this filling in the chicken breasts and secure the edges with a toothpick.
4. Brush the remaining BBQ sauce over the chicken breasts.
5. Place the chicken in the crisper plate and spray them with cooking oil.

6. Return the crisper plate to the Ninja Foodi Dual Zone Air Fryer.
7. Choose the Air Fry mode for Zone 1 and set the temperature to 360 degrees F and the time to 20 minutes.
8. Initiate cooking by pressing the START/STOP button.
9. Serve warm.

Nutrition Info:

- (Per serving) Calories 379 | Fat 19g |Sodium 184mg | Carbs 12.3g | Fiber 0.6g | Sugar 2g | Protein 37.7g

Chicken And Potatoes

Servings: 2
Cooking Time: 10 Minutes
Ingredients:

- 2 potatoes, diced
- 2 chicken breasts, diced
- 4 cloves garlic crushed
- 2 teaspoons smoked paprika
- ½ teaspoon red chili flakes
- 1 teaspoon fresh thyme
- 1 teaspoon salt
- ¼ teaspoon black pepper
- 2 tablespoons olive oil

Directions:

1. Rub chicken with half of the salt, black pepper, oil, thyme, red chili flakes, paprika and garlic.
2. Mix potatoes with remaining spices, oil and garlic in a bowl.
3. Add chicken to one air fryer basket and potatoes the second basket.
4. Return the air fryer basket 1 to Zone 1, and basket 2 to Zone 2 of the Ninja Foodi 2-Basket Air Fryer.
5. Choose the "Air Fry" mode for Zone 1 at 375 degrees F and 10 minutes of cooking time.
6. Select the "MATCH COOK" option to copy the settings for Zone 2.
7. Initiate cooking by pressing the START/PAUSE BUTTON.
8. Flip the chicken and toss potatoes once cooked halfway through.
9. Garnish with chopped parsley.
10. Serve chicken with the potatoes.

Nutrition Info:

- (Per serving) Calories 374 | Fat 13g |Sodium 552mg | Carbs 25g | Fiber 1.2g | Sugar 1.2g | Protein 37.7g

Easy Chicken Thighs

Servings: 8
Cooking Time: 12 Minutes
Ingredients:

- 900g chicken thighs, boneless & skinless
- 2 tsp chilli powder
- 2 tsp olive oil
- 1 tsp garlic powder
- 1 tsp ground cumin
- Pepper
- Salt

Directions:

1. In a bowl, mix chicken with remaining ingredients until well coated.
2. Insert a crisper plate in the Ninja Foodi air fryer baskets.
3. Place chicken thighs in both baskets.
4. Select zone 1 then select "air fry" mode and set the temperature to 390 degrees F for 12 minutes. Press "match" to match zone 2 settings to zone 1. Press "start/stop" to begin. Turn halfway through.

Nutrition Info:

- (Per serving) Calories 230 | Fat 9.7g |Sodium 124mg | Carbs 0.7g | Fiber 0.3g | Sugar 0.2g | Protein 33g

Almond Chicken

Servings: 4
Cooking Time: 25 Minutes
Ingredients:

- 2 large eggs
- ½ cup buttermilk
- 2 teaspoons garlic salt
- 1 teaspoon pepper
- 2 cups slivered almonds, finely chopped
- 4 boneless, skinless chicken breast halves (6 ounces each)

Directions:

1. Whisk together the egg, buttermilk, garlic salt, and pepper in a small bowl.
2. In another small bowl, place the almonds.
3. Dip the chicken in the egg mixture, then roll it in the almonds, patting it down to help the coating stick.
4. Install a crisper plate in both drawers. Place half the chicken breasts in the zone 1 drawer and half in zone 2's, then insert the drawers into the unit.
5. Select zone 1, select AIR FRY, set temperature to 390 degrees F/ 200 degrees C, and set time to 22 minutes. Select MATCH to match zone 2 settings to zone 1. Press the START/STOP button to begin cooking.
6. When the time reaches 11 minutes, press START/STOP to pause the unit. Remove the drawers and flip the chicken. Re-insert the drawers into the unit and press START/STOP to resume cooking.
7. When cooking is complete, remove the chicken.

Nutrition Info:

- (Per serving) Calories 353 | Fat 18g | Sodium 230mg | Carbs 6g | Fiber 2g | Sugar 3g | Protein 41g

Barbecue Chicken Drumsticks With Crispy Kale Chips

Servings:4
Cooking Time: 20 Minutes
Ingredients:

- FOR THE DRUMSTICKS
- 1 tablespoon chili powder
- 2 teaspoons smoked paprika
- ¼ teaspoon kosher salt
- ¼ teaspoon garlic powder
- ¼ teaspoon freshly ground black pepper
- 2 teaspoons dark brown sugar
- 4 chicken drumsticks
- 1 cup barbecue sauce (your favorite)
- FOR THE KALE CHIPS
- 5 cups kale, stems and midribs removed, if needed
- ½ teaspoon garlic powder
- ½ teaspoon kosher salt
- ¼ teaspoon freshly ground black pepper

Directions:

1. To prep the drumsticks: In a small bowl, combine the chili powder, smoked paprika, salt, garlic powder, black pepper, and brown sugar. Rub the spice mixture all over the chicken.
2. To cook the chicken and kale chips: Install a crisper plate in each of the two baskets. Add the chicken drumsticks to the Zone 1 basket and insert the basket in the unit. Add the kale to the Zone 2 basket, sprinkle the kale with the garlic powder, salt, and black pepper and insert the basket in the unit.
3. Select Zone 1, select BAKE, set the temperature to 390°F, and set the time to 20 minutes.
4. Select Zone 2, select AIR FRY, set the temperature to 300°F, and set the time to 15 minutes. Select SMART FINISH.
5. Press START/PAUSE to begin cooking.
6. When the Zone 1 timer reads 5 minutes, press START/PAUSE. Remove the basket and brush the drumsticks with the barbecue sauce. Reinsert the basket and press START/PAUSE to resume cooking.
7. When cooking is complete, the chicken should be cooked through (an instant-read thermometer should read 165°F) and the kale chips will be crispy. Serve hot.

Nutrition Info:

- (Per serving) Calories: 335; Total fat: 11g; Saturated fat: 3g; Carbohydrates: 31g; Fiber: 1.5g; Protein: 26g; Sodium: 1,045mg

Chicken Thighs With Brussels Sprouts

Servings:2
Cooking Time:30
Ingredients:
- 2 tablespoons of honey
- 4 tablespoons of Dijon mustard
- Salt and black pepper, to tat
- 4 tablespoons of olive oil
- 1-1/2 cup Brussels sprouts
- 8 chicken thighs, skinless

Directions:
1. Take a bowl and add chicken thighs to it.
2. Add honey, Dijon mustard, salt, pepper and 2 tablespoons of olive oil to the thighs.
3. Coat the chicken well and marinate it for 1 hour.
4. Now when start cooking season the Brussels sprouts with salt and black pepper along with remaining olive oil.
5. Put the chicken in the zone 1 basket.
6. Put the Brussels sprouts into the zone 2 basket.
7. Select ROAST function for chicken and set time to 30 minutes at 390 degrees F.
8. Select AIR FRY function for Brussels sprouts and set the timer to 20 at 400 degrees F.
9. Once done, serve and enjoy.

Nutrition Info:
- (Per serving) Calories1454 | Fat 72.2g Sodium 869mg | Carbs 23g | Fiber 2.7g | Sugar 19g | Protein 172g

Chicken Wings

Servings:3
Cooking Time:20
Ingredients:
- 1 cup chicken batter mix, Louisiana
- 9 Chicken wings
- ½ teaspoon of smoked paprika
- 2 tablespoons of Dijon mustard
- 1 tablespoon of cayenne pepper
- 1 teaspoon of meat tenderizer, powder
- oil spray, for greasing

Directions:
1. Pat dry chicken wings and add mustard, paprika, meat tenderizer, and cayenne pepper.
2. Dredge it in the chicken batter mix.
3. Oil sprays the chicken wings.
4. Grease both baskets of the air fryer.
5. Divide the wings between the two zones of the air fryer.

6. Set zone 1 to AR FRY mode at 400 degrees F for 20 minutes
7. Select MATCH for zone 2.
8. Hit start to begin with the cooking.
9. Once the cooking cycle complete, serve, and enjoy hot.

Nutrition Info:
- (Per serving) Calories621 | Fat 32.6g Sodium 2016mg | Carbs 46.6g | Fiber 1.1g | Sugar 0.2g | Protein 32.1g

Crumbed Chicken Katsu

Servings: 4
Cooking Time: 26 Minutes.
Ingredients:
- 1 lb. boneless chicken breast, cut in half
- 2 large eggs, beaten
- 1 ½ cups panko bread crumbs
- Salt and black pepper ground to taste
- Cooking spray
- Sauce:
- 1 tablespoon sugar
- 2 tablespoons soy sauce
- 1 tablespoon sherry
- ½ cup ketchup
- 2 teaspoons Worcestershire sauce
- 1 teaspoon garlic, minced

Directions:
1. Mix soy sauce, ketchup, sherry, sugar, garlic, and Worcestershire sauce in a mixing bowl.
2. Keep this katsu aside for a while.
3. Rub the chicken pieces with salt and black pepper.
4. Whisk eggs in a shallow dish and spread breadcrumbs in another tray.
5. Dip the chicken in the egg mixture and coat them with breadcrumbs.
6. Place the coated chicken in the two crisper plates and spray them with cooking spray.
7. Return the crisper plate to the Ninja Foodi Dual Zone Air Fryer.
8. Choose the Air Fry mode for Zone 1 and set the temperature to 390 degrees F and the time to 26 minutes.
9. Select the "MATCH" button to copy the settings for Zone 2.
10. Initiate cooking by pressing the START/STOP button.
11. Flip the chicken once cooked halfway through, then resume cooking.
12. Serve warm with the sauce.

Nutrition Info:
- (Per serving) Calories 220 | Fat 1.7g |Sodium 178mg | Carbs 1.7g | Fiber 0.2g | Sugar 0.2g | Protein 32.9g

Chicken Breast Strips

Servings:2
Cooking Time:22
Ingredients:
- 2 large organic egg
- 1-ounce buttermilk
- 1 cup of cornmeal
- ¼ cup all-purpose flour
- Salt and black pepper, to taste
- 1 pound of chicken breasts, cut into strips
- 2 tablespoons of oil bay seasoning
- oil spray, for greasing

Directions:
1. Take a medium bowl and whisk eggs with buttermilk.
2. In a separate large bowl mix flour, cornmeal, salt, black pepper, and oil bay seasoning.
3. First, dip the chicken breast strip in egg wash and then dredge into the flour mixture.
4. Coat the strip all over and layer on both the baskets that are already grease with oil spray.
5. Grease the chicken breast strips with oil spray as well.
6. Set the zone 1 basket to AIR FRY mode at 400 degrees F for 22 minutes.
7. Select the MATCH button for zone 2.
8. Hit the start button to let the cooking start.
9. Once the cooking cycle is done, serve.

Nutrition Info:
- (Per serving) Calories 788| Fat25g| Sodium835 mg | Carbs60g | Fiber 4.9g| Sugar1.5g | Protein79g

Pretzel Chicken Cordon Bleu

Servings: 4
Cooking Time: 26 Minutes
Ingredients:
- 5 boneless chicken thighs
- 3 cups pretzels, crushed
- 2 eggs, beaten
- 10 deli honey ham, slices
- 5 Swiss cheese slices
- Cooking spray

Directions:
1. Grind pretzels in a food processor.
2. Pound the chicken tights with a mallet.
3. Top each chicken piece with one cheese slice and 2 ham slices.
4. Roll the chicken pieces and secure with a toothpick.
5. Dip the rolls in the eggs and coat with the breadcrumbs.
6. Place these rolls in the air fryer baskets.
7. Spray them with cooking oil.
8. Return the air fryer basket 1 to Zone 1, and basket 2 to Zone 2 of the Ninja Foodi 2-Basket Air Fryer.
9. Choose the "Air Fry" mode for Zone 1 and set the temperature to 375 degrees F and 26 minutes of cooking time.
10. Select the "MATCH COOK" option to copy the settings for Zone 2.
11. Initiate cooking by pressing the START/PAUSE BUTTON.
12. Flip the rolls once cooked halfway through.
13. Serve warm.

Nutrition Info:
- (Per serving) Calories 380 | Fat 29g |Sodium 821mg | Carbs 34.6g | Fiber 0g | Sugar 0g | Protein 30g

Chicken Caprese

Servings: 4
Cooking Time: 10 Minutes
Ingredients:
- 4 chicken breast cutlets
- 1 teaspoon Italian seasoning
- 1 teaspoon salt
- ½ teaspoon black pepper
- 4 slices fresh mozzarella cheese
- 1 large tomato, sliced
- Basil and balsamic vinegar to garnish

Directions:
1. Pat dry the chicken cutlets with a kitchen towel.
2. Rub the chicken with Italian seasoning, black pepper and salt.
3. Place two chicken breasts in each air fryer basket.
4. Return the air fryer basket 1 to Zone 1, and basket 2 to Zone 2 of the Ninja Foodi 2-Basket Air Fryer.
5. Choose the "Air Fry" mode for Zone 1 at 375 degrees F and 10 minutes of cooking time.
6. Select the "MATCH COOK" option to copy the settings for Zone 2.
7. Initiate cooking by pressing the START/PAUSE BUTTON.
8. After 10 minutes top each chicken breast with a slice of cheese and tomato slices.
9. Return the baskets to the Ninja Foodi 2 Baskets Air Fryer and air fry for 5 another minutes.
10. Garnish with balsamic vinegar and basil.
11. Serve warm.

Nutrition Info:
- (Per serving) Calories 502 | Fat 25g |Sodium 230mg | Carbs 1.5g | Fiber 0.2g | Sugar 0.4g | Protein 64.1g

Cornish Hen With Asparagus

Servings: 2
Cooking Time: 45
Ingredients:
- 10 spears of asparagus
- Salt and black pepper, to taste
- 1 Cornish hen
- Salt, to taste
- Black pepper, to taste
- 1 teaspoon of Paprika
- Coconut spray, for greasing
- 2 lemons, sliced

Directions:
1. Wash and pat dry the asparagus and coat it with coconut oil spray.
2. Sprinkle salt on the asparagus and place inside the first basket of the air fryer.
3. Next, take the Cornish hen and rub it well with the salt, black pepper, and paprika.
4. Oil sprays the Cornish hen and place in the second air fryer basket.
5. Press button 1 for the first basket and set it to AIR FRY mode at 350 degrees F, for 8 minutes.
6. For the second basket hit 2 and set the time to 45 minutes at 350 degrees F, by selecting the ROAST mode.
7. To start cooking, hit the smart finish button and press hit start.
8. Once the 6 minutes pass press 1 and pause and take out the asparagus.
9. Once the chicken cooking cycle complete, press 2 and hit pause.
10. Take out the Basket of chicken and let it transfer to the serving plate
11. Serve the chicken with roasted asparagus and slices of lemon.
12. Serve hot and enjoy.

Nutrition Info:
- (Per serving) Calories 192| Fat 4.7g| Sodium 151mg | Carbs10.7 g | Fiber 4.6g | Sugar 3.8g | Protein 30g

Balsamic Duck Breast

Servings: 2
Cooking Time: 20 Minutes.
Ingredients:
- 2 duck breasts
- 1 teaspoon parsley
- Salt and black pepper, to taste
- Marinade:
- 1 tablespoon olive oil
- ½ teaspoon French mustard
- 1 teaspoon dried garlic
- 2 teaspoons honey
- ½ teaspoon balsamic vinegar

Directions:
1. Mix olive oil, mustard, garlic, honey, and balsamic vinegar in a bowl.
2. Add duck breasts to the marinade and rub well.
3. Place one duck breast in each crisper plate.
4. Return the crisper plates to the Ninja Foodi Dual Zone Air Fryer.
5. Choose the Air Fry mode for Zone 1 and set the temperature to 360 degrees F and the time to 20 minutes.
6. Select the "MATCH" button to copy the settings for Zone 2.
7. Initiate cooking by pressing the START/STOP button.
8. Flip the duck breasts once cooked halfway through, then resume cooking.
9. Serve warm.

Nutrition Info:
- (Per serving) Calories 546 | Fat 33.1g |Sodium 1201mg | Carbs 30g | Fiber 2.4g | Sugar 9.7g | Protein 32g

Chicken Potatoes

Servings: 4
Cooking Time: 22 Minutes.
Ingredients:
- 15 ounces canned potatoes drained
- 1 teaspoon olive oil
- 1 teaspoon Lawry's seasoned salt
- ⅛ teaspoons black pepper optional
- 8 ounces boneless chicken breast cubed
- ¼ teaspoon paprika
- ⅜ cup cheddar, shredded
- 4 bacon slices, cooked, cut into strips

Directions:
1. Dice the chicken into small pieces and toss them with olive oil and spices.
2. Drain and dice the potato pieces into smaller cubes.
3. Add potato to the chicken and mix well to coat.
4. Spread the mixture in the two crisper plates in a single layer.
5. Return the crisper plates to the Ninja Foodi Dual Zone Air Fryer.
6. Choose the Air Fry mode for Zone 1 and set the temperature to 390 degrees F and the time to 22 minutes.
7. Select the "MATCH" button to copy the settings for Zone 2.
8. Initiate cooking by pressing the START/STOP button.
9. Top the chicken and potatoes with cheese and bacon.
10. Return the crisper plates to the Ninja Foodi Dual Zone Air Fryer.

11. Select the Max Crisp mode for Zone 1 and set the temperature to 300 degrees F and the time to 5 minutes.

12. Initiate cooking by pressing the START/STOP button.

13. Repeat the same step for Zone 2 to broil the potatoes and chicken in the right drawer.

14. Enjoy with dried herbs on top.

Nutrition Info:

- (Per serving) Calories 346 | Fat 16.1g |Sodium 882mg | Carbs 1.3g | Fiber 0.5g | Sugar 0.5g | Protein 48.2g

Roasted Garlic Chicken Pizza With Cauliflower "wings"

Servings:4

Cooking Time: 25 Minutes

Ingredients:

- FOR THE PIZZA
- 2 prebaked rectangular pizza crusts or flatbreads
- 2 tablespoons olive oil
- 1 tablespoon minced garlic
- 1½ cups shredded part-skim mozzarella cheese
- 6 ounces boneless, skinless chicken breast, thinly sliced
- ¼ teaspoon red pepper flakes (optional)
- FOR THE CAULIFLOWER "WINGS"
- 4 cups cauliflower florets
- 1 tablespoon vegetable oil
- ½ cup Buffalo wing sauce

Directions:

1. To prep the pizza: Trim the pizza crusts to fit in the air fryer basket, if necessary.

2. Brush the top of each crust with the oil and sprinkle with the garlic. Top the crusts with the mozzarella, chicken, and red pepper flakes (if using).

3. To prep the cauliflower "wings": In a large bowl, combine the cauliflower and oil and toss to coat the florets.

4. To cook the pizza and "wings": Install a crisper plate in each of the two baskets. Place one pizza in the Zone 1 basket and insert the basket in the unit. Place the cauliflower in the Zone 2 basket and insert the basket in the unit.

5. Select Zone 1, select ROAST, set the temperature to 375°F, and set the time to 25 minutes.

6. Select Zone 2, select AIR FRY, set the temperature to 390°F, and set the time to 25 minutes. Select SMART FINISH.

7. Press START/PAUSE to begin cooking.

8. When the Zone 1 timer reads 13 minutes, press START/PAUSE. Remove the basket. Transfer the pizza to a cutting board (the chicken should be cooked through and the cheese melted and bubbling). Add the second pizza to the basket. Reinsert the basket in the unit and press START/PAUSE to resume cooking.

9. When the Zone 2 timer reads 5 minutes, press START/PAUSE. Remove the basket and add the Buffalo wing sauce to the cauliflower. Shake well to evenly coat the cauliflower in the sauce. Reinsert the basket and press START/PAUSE to resume cooking.

10. When cooking is complete, the cauliflower will be crisp on the outside and tender inside, and the chicken on the second pizza will be cooked through and the cheese melted.

11. Cut each pizza into 4 slices. Serve with the cauliflower "wings" on the side.

Nutrition Info:

- (Per serving) Calories: 360; Total fat: 20g; Saturated fat: 6.5g; Carbohydrates: 21g; Fiber: 2.5g; Protein: 24g; Sodium: 1,399mg

Buffalo Chicken

Servings: 4

Cooking Time: 22 Minutes

Ingredients:

- ½ cup plain fat-free Greek yogurt
- ¼ cup egg substitute
- 1 tablespoon plus 1 teaspoon hot sauce
- 1 cup panko breadcrumbs
- 1 tablespoon sweet paprika
- 1 tablespoon garlic pepper seasoning
- 1 tablespoon cayenne pepper
- 1-pound skinless, boneless chicken breasts, cut into 1-inch strips

Directions:

1. Combine the Greek yogurt, egg substitute, and hot sauce in a mixing bowl.

2. In a separate bowl, combine the panko breadcrumbs, paprika, garlic powder, and cayenne pepper.

3. Dip the chicken strips in the yogurt mixture, then coat them in the breadcrumb mixture.

4. Install a crisper plate in both drawers. Place the chicken strips into the drawers and then insert the drawers into the unit.

5. Select zone 1, select AIR FRY, set temperature to 390 degrees F/ 200 degrees C, and set time to 22 minutes. Select MATCH to match zone 2 settings to zone 1. Press the START/STOP button to begin cooking.

6. When cooking is complete, serve immediately.

Nutrition Info:

- (Per serving) Calories 234 | Fat 15.8g | Sodium 696mg | Carbs 22.1g | Fiber 1.1g | Sugar 1.7g | Protein 31.2g

Chicken Cordon Bleu

Servings: 4

Cooking Time: 20 Minutes

Ingredients:

- 4 boneless, skinless chicken breast halves (4 ounces each)
- ¼ teaspoon salt
- ¼ teaspoon pepper
- 4 slices deli ham
- 2 slices aged Swiss cheese, halved
- 1 cup panko breadcrumbs
- Cooking spray
- For the sauce:
- 1 tablespoon all-purpose flour
- ½ cup 2% milk
- ¼ cup dry white wine
- 3 tablespoons finely shredded Swiss cheese
- 1/8 teaspoon salt
- Dash pepper

Directions:

1. Season both sides of the chicken breast halves with salt and pepper. You may need to thin the breasts with a mallet.

2. Place 1 slice of ham and half slice of cheese on top of each chicken breast half.

3. Roll the breast up and use toothpicks to secure it.

4. Sprinkle the breadcrumbs on top and spray lightly with the cooking oil.

5. Insert a crisper plate into each drawer. Divide the chicken between each drawer and insert the drawers into the unit.

6. Select zone 1, select AIR FRY, set temperature to 390 degrees F/ 200 degrees C, and set time to 7 minutes. Select MATCH to match zone 2 settings to zone 1. Press the START/STOP button to begin cooking.

7. When the time reaches 5 minutes, press START/STOP to pause the unit. Remove the drawers and flip the chicken. Re-insert the drawers into the unit and press START/STOP to resume cooking.

8. To make the sauce, mix the flour, wine, and milk together in a small pot until smooth. Bring to a boil over high heat, stirring frequently, for 1–2 minutes, or until the sauce has thickened.

9. Reduce the heat to medium. Add the cheese. Cook and stir for 2–3 minutes, or until the cheese has melted and the sauce has thickened and bubbled. Add salt and pepper to taste. Keep the sauce heated at a low temperature until ready to serve.

Nutrition Info:

- (Per serving) Calories 272 | Fat 8g | Sodium 519mg | Carbs 14g | Fiber 2g | Sugar 1g | Protein 32g

Beef, Pork, And Lamb Recipes

Korean Bbq Beef

Servings: 6
Cooking Time: 30 Minutes
Ingredients:

- For the meat:
- 1 pound flank steak or thinly sliced steak
- ¼ cup corn starch
- Coconut oil spray
- For the sauce:
- ½ cup soy sauce or gluten-free soy sauce
- ½ cup brown sugar
- 2 tablespoons white wine vinegar
- 1 clove garlic, crushed
- 1 tablespoon hot chili sauce
- 1 teaspoon ground ginger
- ½ teaspoon sesame seeds
- 1 tablespoon corn starch
- 1 tablespoon water

Directions:

1. To begin, prepare the steak. Thinly slice it in that toss it in the corn starch to be coated thoroughly. Spray the tops with some coconut oil.
2. Spray the crisping plates and drawers with the coconut oil.
3. Place the crisping plates into the drawers. Place the steak strips into each drawer. Insert both drawers into the unit.
4. Select zone 1, Select AIR FRY, set the temperature to 375 degrees F/ 190 degrees C, and set time to 30 minutes. Select MATCH to match zone 2 settings with zone 1. Press the START/STOP button to begin cooking.
5. While the steak is cooking, add the sauce ingredients EXCEPT for the corn starch and water to a medium saucepan.
6. Warm it up to a low boil, then whisk in the corn starch and water.
7. Carefully remove the steak and pour the sauce over. Mix well.

Nutrition Info:

- (Per serving) Calories 500 | Fat 19.8g | Sodium 680mg | Carbs 50.1g | Fiber 4.1g | Sugar 0g | Protein 27.9g

Bell Peppers With Sausages

Servings:4
Cooking Time:20
Ingredients:

- 6 beef or pork Italian sausages
- 4 bell peppers, whole
- Oil spray, for greasing
- 2 cups of cooked rice
- 1 cup of sour cream

Directions:

1. Put the bell pepper in the zone 1 basket and sausages in the zone 2 basket of the air fryer.
2. Set zone 1 to AIR FRY MODE for 10 minutes at 400 degrees F.
3. For zone 2 set it to 20 minutes at 375 degrees F.
4. Hit the smart finish button, so both finish at the same time.
5. After 5 minutes take out the sausage basket and break or mince it with a plastic spatula.
6. Then, let the cooking cycle finish.
7. Once done serve the minced meat with bell peppers and serve over cooked rice with a dollop of sour cream.

Nutrition Info:

- (Per serving) Calories1356 | Fat 81.2g| Sodium 3044 mg | Carbs 96g | Fiber 3.1g | Sugar 8.3g | Protein 57.2 g

Air Fryer Meatloaves

Servings: 4
Cooking Time: 22 Minutes.
Ingredients:

- ⅓ cup milk
- 2 tablespoons basil pesto
- 1 egg, beaten
- 1 garlic clove, minced
- ¼ teaspoons black pepper
- 1 lb. ground beef
- ⅓ cup panko bread crumbs
- 8 pepperoni slices
- ½ cup marinara sauce, warmed
- 1 tablespoon fresh basil, chopped

Directions:

1. Mix pesto, milk, egg, garlic, and black pepper in a medium-sized bowl.
2. Stir in ground beef and bread crumbs, then mix.
3. Make the 4 small-sized loaves with this mixture and top them with 2 pepperoni slices.
4. Press the slices into the meatloaves.
5. Place the meatloaves in the two crisper plates.
6. Return the crisper plate to the Ninja Foodi Dual Zone Air Fryer.
7. Choose the Air Fry mode for Zone 1 and set the temperature to 390 degrees F and the time to 22 minutes.
8. Select the "MATCH" button to copy the settings for Zone 2.
9. Initiate cooking by pressing the START/STOP button.
10. Top them with marinara sauce and basil to serve.
11. Serve warm.

Nutrition Info:

- (Per serving) Calories 316 | Fat 12.2g |Sodium 587mg | Carbs 12.2g | Fiber 1g | Sugar 1.8g | Protein 25.8g

Beef Kofta Kebab

Servings: 4
Cooking Time: 18 Minutes
Ingredients:

- 455g ground beef
- ¼ cup white onion, grated
- ¼ cup parsley, chopped
- 1 tablespoon mint, chopped
- 2 cloves garlic, minced
- 1 teaspoon salt
- ½ teaspoon cumin
- 1 teaspoon oregano
- ½ teaspoon garlic salt
- 1 egg

Directions:

1. Mix ground beef with onion, parsley, mint, garlic, cumin, oregano, garlic salt and egg in a bowl.
2. Take 3 tbsp-sized beef kebabs out of this mixture
3. Place the kebabs in the air fryer baskets.
4. Return the air fryer basket 1 to Zone 1, and basket 2 to Zone 2 of the Ninja Foodi 2-Basket Air Fryer.
5. Choose the "Air Fry" mode for Zone 1 at 375 degrees F and 18 minutes of cooking time.
6. Select the "MATCH COOK" option to copy the settings for Zone 2.
7. Initiate cooking by pressing the START/PAUSE BUTTON.
8. Flip the kebabs once cooked halfway through.
9. Serve warm.

Nutrition Info:

- (Per serving) Calories 316 | Fat 12.2g |Sodium 587mg | Carbs 12.2g | Fiber 1g | Sugar 1.8g | Protein 25.8g

Beef Ribs Ii

Servings:2
Cooking Time:1
Ingredients:

- ¼ cup olive oil
- 4 garlic cloves, minced
- ½ cup white wine vinegar
- ¼ cup soy sauce, reduced-sodium
- ¼ cup Worcestershire sauce
- 1 lemon juice
- Salt and black pepper, to taste
- 2 tablespoons of Italian seasoning
- 1 teaspoon of smoked paprika

- 2 tablespoons of mustard
- ½ cup maple syrup
- Meat Ingredients:
- Oil spray, for greasing
- 8 beef ribs lean

Directions:

1. Take a large bowl and add all the ingredients under marinade ingredients.
2. Put the marinade in a zip lock bag and add ribs to it.
3. Let it sit for 4 hours.
4. Now take out the basket of air fryer and grease the baskets with oil spray.
5. Now dived the ribs among two baskets.
6. Set it to AIR fry mode at 220 degrees F for 30 minutes.
7. Select Pause and take out the baskets.
8. Afterward, flip the ribs and cook for 30 minutes at 250 degrees F.
9. Once done, serve the juicy and tender ribs.
10. Enjoy.

Nutrition Info:

- (Per serving) Calories 1927| Fat116g| Sodium 1394mg | Carbs 35.2g | Fiber 1.3g| Sugar29 g | Protein 172.3g

Chinese Bbq Pork

Servings:35
Cooking Time:25
Ingredients:

- 4 tablespoons of soy sauce
- ¼ cup red wine
- 2 tablespoons of oyster sauce
- ¼ tablespoons of hoisin sauce
- ¼ cup honey
- ¼ cup brown sugar
- Pinch of salt
- Pinch of black pepper
- 1 teaspoon of ginger garlic, paste
- 1 teaspoon of five-spice powder
- 1.5 pounds of pork shoulder, sliced

Directions:

1. Take a bowl and mix all the ingredients listed under sauce ingredients.
2. Transfer half of it to a sauce pan and let it cook for 10 minutes.
3. Set it aside.
4. Let the pork marinate in the remaining sauce for 2 hours.
5. Afterward, put the pork slices in the basket and set it to AIRBORIL mode 450 degrees for 25 minutes.
6. Make sure the internal temperature is above 160 degrees F once cooked.
7. If not add a few more minutes to the overall cooking time.

8. Once done, take it out and baste it with prepared sauce.

9. Serve and Enjoy.

Nutrition Info:

- (Per serving) Calories 1239| Fat 73 g| Sodium 2185 mg | Carbs 57.3 g | Fiber 0.4g| Sugar53.7 g | Protein 81.5 g

Air Fried Lamb Chops

Servings: 4

Cooking Time: 10 Minutes

Ingredients:

- 700g lamb chops
- ½ teaspoon oregano
- 3 tablespoons parsley, minced
- ½ teaspoon black pepper
- 3 cloves garlic minced
- 2 tablespoons lemon juice
- 2 tablespoons olive oil
- Salt to taste

Directions:

1. Pat dry the chops and mix with lemon juice and the rest of the ingredients.

2. Place these chops in the air fryer baskets.

3. Return the air fryer basket 1 to Zone 1, and basket 2 to Zone 2 of the Ninja Foodi 2-Basket Air Fryer.

4. Choose the "Air Fry" mode for Zone 1and set the temperature to 400 degrees F and 10 minutes of cooking time.

5. Select the "MATCH COOK" option to copy the settings for Zone 2.

6. Initiate cooking by pressing the START/PAUSE BUTTON.

7. Flip the pork chops once cooked halfway through.

8. Serve warm.

Nutrition Info:

- (Per serving) Calories 396 | Fat 23.2g |Sodium 622mg | Carbs 0.7g | Fiber 0g | Sugar 0g | Protein 45.6g

Pork Chops

Servings:2

Cooking Time:17

Ingredients:

- 1 tablespoon of rosemary, chopped
- Salt and black pepper, to taste
- 2 garlic cloves
- 1-inch ginger
- 2 tablespoons of olive oil
- 8 pork chops

Directions:

1. Take a blender and pulse together rosemary, salt, pepper, garlic cloves, ginger, and olive oil.

2. Rub this marinade over pork chops and let it rest for 1 hour.

3. Then divide it amongst air fryer baskets and set it to AIR FRY mode for 17 minutes at 375 degrees F.

4. Once the cooking cycle is done, take out and serve hot.

Nutrition Info:

- (Per serving) Calories 1154| Fat 93.8g| Sodium 225mg | Carbs 2.1g | Fiber0.8 g | Sugar 0g | Protein 72.2g

Steak In Air Fry

Servings:1

Cooking Time:20

Ingredients:

- 2 teaspoons of canola oil
- 1 tablespoon of Montreal steaks seasoning
- 1 pound of beef steak

Directions:

1. The first step is to season the steak on both sides with canola oil and then rub a generous amount of steak seasoning all over.

2. We are using the AIR BROIL feature of the ninja air fryer and it works with one basket.

3. Put the steak in the basket and set it to AIR BROIL at 450 degrees F for 20 -22 minutes.

4. After 7 minutes, hit pause and take out the basket to flip the steak, and cover it with foil on top, for the remaining 14 minutes.

5. Once done, serve the medium-rare steak and enjoy it by resting for 10 minutes.

6. Serve by cutting in slices.

7. Enjoy.

Nutrition Info:

- (Per serving) Calories 935| Fat 37.2g| Sodium 1419mg | Carbs 0g | Fiber 0g| Sugar 0g | Protein137.5 g

Tomahawk Steak

Servings: 4

Cooking Time: 12 Minutes

Ingredients:

- 4 tablespoons butter, softened
- 2 cloves garlic, minced
- 2 teaspoons chopped fresh parsley
- 1 teaspoon chopped chives
- 1 teaspoon chopped fresh thyme
- 1 teaspoon chopped fresh rosemary
- 2 (2 pounds each) bone-in ribeye steaks
- Kosher salt, to taste
- Freshly ground black pepper, to taste

Directions:

1. In a small bowl, combine the butter and herbs. Place the mixture in the center of a piece of plastic wrap and roll it into a log. Twist the ends together to keep it tight and refrigerate until hardened, about 20 minutes.

2. Season the steaks on both sides with salt and pepper.

3. Install a crisper plate in both drawers. Place one steak in the zone 1 drawer and one in zone 2's, then insert the drawers into the unit.

4. Select zone 1, select AIR FRY, set temperature to 390 degrees F/ 200 degrees C, and set time to 12 minutes. Select MATCH to match zone 2 settings to zone 1. Press the START/STOP button to begin cooking.

5. When the time reaches 10 minutes, press START/STOP to pause the unit. Remove the drawers and flip the steaks. Add the herb-butter to the tops of the steaks. Re-insert the drawers into the unit and press START/STOP to resume cooking.

6. Serve and enjoy!

Nutrition Info:

- (Per serving) Calories 338 | Fat 21.2g | Sodium 1503mg | Carbs 5.1g | Fiber 0.3g | Sugar 4.6g | Protein 29.3g

Pork Chops And Potatoes

Servings: 3

Cooking Time: 12 Minutes

Ingredients:

- 455g red potatoes
- Olive oil
- Salt and pepper
- 1 teaspoon garlic powder
- 1 teaspoon fresh rosemary, chopped
- 2 tablespoons brown sugar
- 1 tablespoon soy sauce
- 1 tablespoon Worcestershire sauce
- 1 teaspoon lemon juice
- 3 small pork chops

Directions:

1. Mix potatoes and pork chops with remaining ingredients in a bowl.

2. Divide the ingredients in the air fryer baskets.

3. Return the air fryer basket 1 to Zone 1, and basket 2 to Zone 2 of the Ninja Foodi 2-Basket Air Fryer.

4. Choose the "Air Fry" mode for Zone 1 at 400 degrees F and 12 minutes of cooking time.

5. Select the "MATCH COOK" option to copy the settings for Zone 2.

6. Initiate cooking by pressing the START/PAUSE BUTTON.

7. Flip the chops and toss potatoes once cooked halfway through.

8. Serve warm.

Nutrition Info:

- (Per serving) Calories 352 | Fat 9.1g | Sodium 1294mg | Carbs 3.9g | Fiber 1g | Sugar 1g | Protein 61g

Beef Ribs I

Servings:2

Cooking Time:15

Ingredients:

- 4 tablespoons of barbecue spice rub
- 1 tablespoon kosher salt and black pepper
- 3 tablespoons brown sugar
- 2 pounds of beef ribs (3-3 1/2 pounds), cut in thirds
- 1 cup barbecue sauce

Directions:

1. In a small bowl, add salt, pepper, brown sugar, and BBQ spice rub.

2. Grease the ribs with oil spray from both sides and then rub it with a spice mixture.

3. Divide the ribs amongst the basket and set it to AIR FRY MODE at 375 degrees F for 15 minutes.

4. Hit start and let the air fryer cook the ribs.

5. Once done, serve with the coating BBQ sauce.

Nutrition Info:

- (Per serving) Calories1081 | Fat 28.6 g| Sodium 1701mg | Carbs 58g | Fiber 0.8g| Sugar 45.7g | Protein 138 g

Pork Chops With Brussels Sprouts

Servings: 4

Cooking Time: 15 Minutes.

Ingredients:

- 4 bone-in center-cut pork chop
- Cooking spray
- Salt, to taste
- Black pepper, to taste
- 2 teaspoons olive oil
- 2 teaspoons pure maple syrup
- 2 teaspoons Dijon mustard
- 6 ounces Brussels sprouts, quartered

Directions:

1. Rub pork chop with salt, ¼ teaspoons black pepper, and cooking spray.

2. Toss Brussels sprouts with mustard, syrup, oil, ¼ teaspoon of black pepper in a medium bowl.

3. Add pork chop to the crisper plate of Zone 1 of the Ninja Foodi Dual Zone Air Fryer.

4. Return the crisper plate to the Ninja Foodi Dual Zone Air Fryer.

5. Choose the Air Fry mode for Zone 1 and set the temperature to 400 degrees F and the time to 15 minutes.

6. Add the Brussels sprouts to the crisper plate of Zone 2 and return it to the unit.

7. Choose the Air Fry mode for Zone 2 with 350 degrees F and the time to 13 minutes.

8. Press the SYNC button to sync the finish time for both Zones.

9. Initiate cooking by pressing the START/STOP button.

10. Serve warm and fresh

Nutrition Info:

- (Per serving) Calories 336 | Fat 27.1g |Sodium 66mg | Carbs 1.1g | Fiber 0.4g | Sugar 0.2g | Protein 19.7g

Turkey And Beef Meatballs

Servings: 6

Cooking Time: 24 Minutes.

Ingredients:

- 1 medium shallot, minced
- 2 tablespoons olive oil
- 3 garlic cloves, minced
- ¼ cup panko crumbs
- 2 tablespoons whole milk
- ⅔ lb. lean ground beef
- ⅓ lb. bulk turkey sausage
- 1 large egg, lightly beaten
- ¼ cup parsley, chopped
- 1 tablespoon fresh thyme, chopped
- 1 tablespoon fresh rosemary, chopped
- 1 tablespoon Dijon mustard
- ½ teaspoon salt

Directions:

1. Preheat your oven to 400 degrees F. Place a medium non-stick pan over medium-high heat.

2. Add oil and shallot, then sauté for 2 minutes.

3. Toss in the garlic and cook for 1 minute.

4. Remove this pan from the heat.

5. Whisk panko with milk in a large bowl and leave it for 5 minutes.

6. Add cooked shallot mixture and mix well.

7. Stir in egg, parsley, turkey sausage, beef, thyme, rosemary, salt, and mustard.

8. Mix well, then divide the mixture into 1 ½-inch balls.

9. Divide these balls into the two crisper plates and spray them with cooking oil.

10. Return the crisper plates to the Ninja Foodi Dual Zone Air Fryer.

11. Choose the Air Fry mode for Zone 1 and set the temperature to 400 degrees F and the time to 21 minutes.

12. Select the "MATCH" button to copy the settings for Zone 2.

13. Initiate cooking by pressing the START/STOP button.

14. Serve warm.

Nutrition Info:

- (Per serving) Calories 551 | Fat 31g |Sodium 1329mg | Carbs 1.5g | Fiber 0.8g | Sugar 0.4g | Protein 64g

Italian-style Meatballs With Garlicky Roasted Broccoli

Servings:4

Cooking Time: 15 Minutes

Ingredients:

- FOR THE MEATBALLS
- 1 large egg
- ¼ cup Italian-style bread crumbs
- 1 pound ground beef (85 percent lean)
- ¼ cup grated Parmesan cheese
- ¼ teaspoon kosher salt
- Nonstick cooking spray
- 2 cups marinara sauce
- FOR THE ROASTED BROCCOLI
- 4 cups broccoli florets
- 1 tablespoon olive oil
- ¼ teaspoon kosher salt
- ¼ teaspoon freshly ground pepper
- ¼ teaspoon red pepper flakes
- 1 tablespoon minced garlic

Directions:

1. To prep the meatballs: In a large bowl, beat the egg. Mix in the bread crumbs and let sit for 5 minutes.

2. Add the beef, Parmesan, and salt and mix until just combined. Form the meatball mixture into 8 meatballs, about 1 inch in diameter. Mist with cooking spray.

3. To prep the broccoli: In a large bowl, combine the broccoli, olive oil, salt, black pepper, and red pepper flakes. Toss to coat the broccoli evenly.

4. To cook the meatballs and broccoli: Install a crisper plate in the Zone 1 basket. Place the meatballs in the basket and insert the basket in the unit. Place the broccoli in the Zone 2 basket, sprinkle the garlic over the broccoli, and insert the basket in the unit.

5. Select Zone 1, select AIR FRY, set the temperature to 400°F, and set the time to 12 minutes.

6. Select Zone 2, select ROAST, set the temperature to 390°F, and set the time to 15 minutes. Select SMART FINISH.

7. Press START/PAUSE to begin cooking.

8. When the Zone 1 timer reads 5 minutes, press START/PAUSE. Remove the basket and pour the marinara sauce over the meatballs. Reinsert the basket and press START/PAUSE to resume cooking.

9. When cooking is complete, the meatballs should be cooked through and the broccoli will have begun to brown on the edges.

Nutrition Info:

- (Per serving) Calories: 493; Total fat: 33g; Saturated fat: 9g; Carbohydrates: 24g; Fiber: 3g; Protein: 31g; Sodium: 926mg

Beef And Bean Taquitos With Mexican Rice

Servings:4
Cooking Time: 15 Minutes
Ingredients:

- FOR THE TAQUITOS
- ½ pound ground beef (85 percent lean)
- 1 tablespoon taco seasoning
- 8 (6-inch) soft white corn tortillas
- Nonstick cooking spray
- ¾ cup canned refried beans
- ½ cup shredded Mexican blend cheese (optional)
- FOR THE MEXICAN RICE
- 1 cup dried instant white rice (not microwavable)
- 1½ cups chicken broth
- ¼ cup jarred salsa
- 2 tablespoons canned tomato sauce
- 1 tablespoon vegetable oil
- ½ teaspoon kosher salt

Directions:

1. To prep the taquitos: In a large bowl, mix the ground beef and taco seasoning until well combined.
2. Mist both sides of each tortilla lightly with cooking spray.
3. To prep the Mexican rice: In the Zone 2 basket, combine the rice, broth, salsa, tomato sauce, oil, and salt. Stir well to ensure all of the rice is submerged in the liquid.
4. To cook the taquitos and rice: Install a crisper plate in the Zone 1 basket. Place the seasoned beef in the basket and insert the basket in the unit. Insert the Zone 2 basket in the unit.
5. Select Zone 1, select AIR FRY, set the temperature to 390°F, and set the time to 15 minutes.
6. Select Zone 2, select BAKE, set the temperature to 350°F, and set the time to 10 minutes. Select SMART FINISH.
7. Press START/PAUSE to begin cooking.
8. When the Zone 1 timer reads 10 minutes, press START/PAUSE. Remove the basket and transfer the beef to a medium bowl. Add the refried beans and cheese (if using) and combine well. Spoon 2 tablespoons of the filling onto each tortilla and roll tightly. Place the taquitos in the Zone 1 basket seam-side down. Reinsert the basket in the unit and press START/PAUSE to resume cooking.
9. When cooking is complete, the taquitos should be crisp and golden brown and the rice cooked through. Serve hot.

Nutrition Info:

- (Per serving) Calories: 431; Total fat: 13g; Saturated fat: 4g; Carbohydrates: 52g; Fiber: 5.5g; Protein: 18g; Sodium: 923mg

Breaded Pork Chops

Servings: 4
Cooking Time: 10 Minutes
Ingredients:

- 4 boneless, center-cut pork chops, 1-inch thick
- 1 teaspoon Cajun seasoning
- 1½ cups cheese and garlic-flavored croutons
- 2 eggs
- Cooking spray

Directions:

1. Season both sides of the pork chops with the Cajun seasoning on a platter.
2. In a small food processor, pulse the croutons until finely chopped; transfer to a shallow plate.
3. In a separate shallow bowl, lightly beat the eggs.
4. Dip the pork chops in the egg, allowing any excess to drip off. Then place the chops in the crouton crumbs. Coat the chops in cooking spray.
5. Install a crisper plate in both drawers. Place half the pork chops in the zone 1 drawer and half in zone 2's, then insert the drawers into the unit.
6. Select zone 1, select ROAST, set temperature to 390 degrees F/ 200 degrees C, and set time to 10 minutes. Select MATCH to match zone 2 settings to zone 1. Press the START/STOP button to begin cooking.
7. When the time reaches 6 minutes, press START/STOP to pause the unit. Remove the drawers and flip the chops. Reinsert the drawers into the unit and press START/STOP to resume cooking.
8. When cooking is complete, serve and enjoy!

Nutrition Info:

- (Per serving) Calories 394 | Fat 18.1g | Sodium 428mg | Carbs 10g | Fiber 0.8g | Sugar 0.9g | Protein 44.7g

Pork Chops With Apples

Servings: 2
Cooking Time: 15 Minutes
Ingredients:

- ½ small red cabbage, sliced
- 1 apple, sliced
- 1 sweet onion, sliced
- 2 tablespoons oil
- ½ teaspoon cumin
- ½ teaspoon paprika
- Salt and black pepper, to taste
- 2 boneless pork chops (1″ thick)

Directions:

1. Toss pork chops with apple and the rest of the ingredients in a bowl.
2. Divide the mixture in the air fryer baskets.

3. Return the air fryer basket 1 to Zone 1, and basket 2 to Zone 2 of the Ninja Foodi 2-Basket Air Fryer.

4. Choose the "Air Fry" mode for Zone 1 and set the temperature to 400 degrees F and 15 minutes of cooking time.

5. Select the "MATCH COOK" option to copy the settings for Zone 2.

6. Initiate cooking by pressing the START/PAUSE BUTTON.

7. Serve warm.

Nutrition Info:

- (Per serving) Calories 374 | Fat 25g |Sodium 275mg | Carbs 7.3g | Fiber 0g | Sugar 6g | Protein 12.3g

Mongolian Beef With Sweet Chili Brussels Sprouts

Servings:4
Cooking Time: 20 Minutes

Ingredients:

- FOR THE MONGOLIAN BEEF
- 1 pound flank steak, cut into thin strips
- 1 tablespoon olive oil
- 2 tablespoons cornstarch
- ½ cup reduced-sodium soy sauce
- ½ cup packed light brown sugar
- 1 tablespoon chili paste (optional)
- 1 tablespoon minced garlic
- 1 tablespoon minced fresh ginger
- 2 scallions, chopped
- FOR THE BRUSSELS SPROUTS
- 1 pound Brussels sprouts, halved lengthwise
- 1 tablespoon olive oil
- ½ cup gochujang sauce
- 2 tablespoons rice vinegar
- 1 tablespoon reduced-sodium soy sauce
- 1 tablespoon light brown sugar
- 1 teaspoon fresh garlic

Directions:

1. To prep the Mongolian beef: In a large bowl, combine the flank steak and olive oil and toss to coat. Add the cornstarch and toss to coat.

2. In a small bowl, whisk together the soy sauce, brown sugar, chili paste (if using), garlic, and ginger. Set the soy sauce mixture aside.

3. To prep the Brussels sprouts: In a large bowl, combine the Brussels sprouts and oil and toss to coat.

4. In a small bowl, whisk together the gochujang sauce, vinegar, soy sauce, brown sugar, and garlic. Set the chili sauce mixture aside.

5. To cook the beef and Brussels sprouts: Install a crisper plate in each of the two baskets. Place the beef in the Zone 1

basket and insert the basket in the unit. Place the Brussels sprouts in the Zone 2 basket and insert the basket in the unit.

6. Select Zone 1, select AIR FRY, set the temperature to 390°F, and set the time to 15 minutes.

7. Select Zone 2, select AIR FRY, set the temperature to 400°F, and set the time to 20 minutes. Select SMART FINISH.

8. Press START/PAUSE to begin cooking.

9. When both timers read 5 minutes, press START/PAUSE. Remove the Zone 1 basket, add the reserved soy sauce mixture and the scallions, and toss with the beef. Reinsert the basket. Remove the Zone 2 basket, add the reserved chili sauce mixture, and toss with the Brussels sprouts. Reinsert the basket and press START/PAUSE to resume cooking.

10. When cooking is complete, the steak should be cooked through and the Brussels sprouts tender and slightly caramelized. Serve warm.

Nutrition Info:

- (Per serving) Calories: 481; Total fat: 16g; Saturated fat: 4.5g; Carbohydrates: 60g; Fiber: 5g; Protein: 27g; Sodium: 2,044mg

Tender Pork Chops

Servings: 2
Cooking Time: 20 Minutes

Ingredients:

- 2 pork chops
- 1 tsp dry mustard
- 1 tsp ground coriander
- 1 tbsp chilli powder
- 30ml olive oil
- ¼ tsp cayenne
- ½ tsp ground cumin
- 1 tsp smoked paprika
- Pepper
- Salt

Directions:

1. In a small bowl, mix chilli powder, paprika, cayenne, coriander, mustard, pepper, and salt.

2. Brush the pork chops with oil and rub with spice mixture.

3. Insert a crisper plate in the Ninja Foodi air fryer baskets.

4. Place the chops in both baskets.

5. Select zone 1, then select "air fry" mode and set the temperature to 375 degrees F for 10 minutes. Press "match" to match zone 2 settings to zone 1. Press "start/stop" to begin. Turn halfway through.

Nutrition Info:

- (Per serving) Calories 401 | Fat 35.3g |Sodium 173mg | Carbs 3.6g | Fiber 2g | Sugar 0.5g | Protein 19.1g

Tasty Pork Skewers

Servings: 3

Cooking Time: 10 Minutes

Ingredients:

- 450g pork shoulder, cut into ¼-inch pieces
- 66ml soy sauce
- ½ tbsp garlic, crushed
- 1 tbsp ginger paste
- 1 ½ tsp sesame oil
- 22ml rice vinegar
- 21ml honey
- Pepper
- Salt

Directions:

1. In a bowl, mix meat with the remaining ingredients. Cover and place in the refrigerator for 30 minutes.
2. Thread the marinated meat onto the soaked skewers.
3. Insert a crisper plate in the Ninja Foodi air fryer baskets.
4. Place the pork skewers in both baskets.
5. Select zone 1, then select "air fry" mode and set the temperature to 360 degrees F for 10 minutes. Press "match" and then press "start/stop" to begin. Turn halfway through.

Nutrition Info:

- (Per serving) Calories 520 | Fat 34.7g |Sodium 1507mg | Carbs 12.2g | Fiber 0.5g | Sugar 9.1g | Protein 37g

Tasty Lamb Patties

Servings: 8

Cooking Time: 12 Minutes

Ingredients:

- 900g ground lamb
- 1 tbsp ground coriander
- 4g fresh parsley, chopped
- 1 tsp garlic, minced
- ½ tsp cinnamon
- 1 tsp paprika
- 1 tbsp ground cumin
- Pepper
- Salt

Directions:

1. Add ground meat and remaining ingredients into a bowl and mix until well combined.
2. Insert a crisper plate in the Ninja Foodi air fryer baskets.
3. Make patties from the meat mixture and place in both baskets.
4. Select zone 1, then select "air fry" mode and set the temperature to 390 degrees F for 12 minutes. Press "match" to match zone 2 settings to zone 1. Press "start/stop" to begin. Turn halfway through.

Nutrition Info:

- (Per serving) Calories 216 | Fat 8.5g |Sodium 108mg | Carbs 0.8g | Fiber 0.3g | Sugar 0.1g | Protein 32.1g

Lamb Chops With Dijon Garlic

Servings: 4

Cooking Time: 22 Minutes

Ingredients:

- 2 teaspoons Dijon mustard
- 2 teaspoons olive oil
- 1 teaspoon soy sauce
- 1 teaspoon garlic, minced
- 1 teaspoon cumin powder
- 1 teaspoon cayenne pepper
- 1 teaspoon Italian spice blend (optional)
- ¼ teaspoon salt
- 8 lamb chops

Directions:

1. Combine the Dijon mustard, olive oil, soy sauce, garlic, cumin powder, cayenne pepper, Italian spice blend (optional), and salt in a medium mixing bowl.
2. Put the marinade in a large Ziploc bag. Add the lamb chops. Seal the bag tightly after pressing out the air. Coat the lamb in the marinade by shaking the bag and pressing the chops into the mixture. Place in the fridge for at least 30 minutes, or up to overnight, to marinate.
3. Install a crisper plate in both drawers. Place half the lamb chops in the zone 1 drawer and half in zone 2's, then insert the drawers into the unit.
4. Select zone 1, select AIR FRY, set temperature to 390 degrees F/ 200 degrees C, and set time to 22 minutes. Select MATCH to match zone 2 settings to zone 1. Press the START/STOP button to begin cooking.
5. When the time reaches 11 minutes, press START/STOP to pause the unit. Remove the drawers and flip the lamb chops. Re-insert the drawers into the unit and press START/STOP to resume cooking.
6. Serve and enjoy!

Nutrition Info:

- (Per serving) Calories 343 | Fat 15.1g | Sodium 380mg | Carbs 0.9 g | Fiber 0.3g | Sugar 0.1g | Protein 48.9g

Steak And Asparagus Bundles

Servings: 6
Cooking Time: 10 Minutes

Ingredients:

- 907g flank steak, cut into 6 pieces
- Salt and black pepper, to taste
- ½ cup tamari sauce
- 2 cloves garlic, crushed
- 455g asparagus, trimmed
- 3 capsicums, sliced
- ¼ cup balsamic vinegar
- 79 ml beef broth
- 2 tablespoons unsalted butter
- Olive oil spray

Directions:

1. Mix steaks with black pepper, tamari sauce, and garlic in a Ziplock bag.
2. Seal the bag, shake well and refrigerate for 1 hour.
3. Place the steaks on the working surface and top each with asparagus and capsicums.
4. Roll the steaks and secure them with toothpicks.
5. Place these rolls in the air fryer baskets.
6. Return the air fryer basket 1 to Zone 1, and basket 2 to Zone 2 of the Ninja Foodi 2-Basket Air Fryer.
7. Choose the "Air Fry" mode for Zone 1 and set the temperature to 400 degrees F and 10 minutes of cooking time.
8. Select the "MATCH COOK" option to copy the settings for Zone 2.
9. Initiate cooking by pressing the START/PAUSE BUTTON.
10. Meanwhile, cook broth with butter and vinegar in a saucepan.
11. Cook this mixture until reduced by half and adjust seasoning with black pepper and salt.
12. Serve the steak rolls with the prepared sauce.

Nutrition Info:

- (Per serving) Calories 551 | Fat 31g |Sodium 1329mg | Carbs 1½g | Fiber 0.8g | Sugar 0.4g | Protein 64g

Garlic Sirloin Steak

Servings: 4
Cooking Time: 10 Minutes

Ingredients:

- 4 sirloin steak
- 30ml olive oil
- 28g steak sauce
- ½ tsp ground coriander
- 1 tsp garlic, minced
- 1 tbsp thyme, chopped
- Pepper
- Salt

Directions:

1. In a bowl, mix steak with thyme, oil, steak sauce, coriander, garlic, pepper, and salt. Cover and set aside for 2 hours.
2. Insert a crisper plate in Ninja Foodi air fryer baskets.
3. Place the marinated steaks in both baskets.
4. Select zone 1 then select air fry mode and set the temperature to 360 degrees F for 10 minutes. Press "match" and then "start/stop" to begin.

Nutrition Info:

- (Per serving) Calories 348 | Fat 18.1g |Sodium 39mg | Carbs 0.7g | Fiber 0.3g | Sugar 0g | Protein 0.1g

Fish And Seafood Recipes

Bang Bang Shrimp

Servings: 4

Cooking Time: 20 Minutes

Ingredients:

- For the shrimp:
- 1 cup corn starch
- Salt and pepper, to taste
- 2 pounds shrimp, peeled and deveined
- ½ to 1 cup buttermilk
- Cooking oil spray
- 1 large egg whisked with 1 teaspoon water
- For the sauce:
- 1/3 cup sweet Thai chili sauce
- ¼ cup sour cream
- ¼ cup mayonnaise
- 2 tablespoons buttermilk
- 1 tablespoon sriracha, or to taste
- Pinch dried dill weed

Directions:

1. Season the corn starch with salt and pepper in a wide, shallow bowl.
2. In a large mixing bowl, toss the shrimp in the buttermilk to coat them.
3. Dredge the shrimp in the seasoned corn starch.
4. Brush with the egg wash after spraying with cooking oil.
5. Place a crisper plate in each drawer. Place the shrimp in a single layer in each. You may need to cook in batches.
6. Select zone 1, then AIR FRY, then set the temperature to 360 degrees F/ 180 degrees C with a 5-minute timer. To match zone 2 settings to zone 1, choose MATCH. To begin, select START/STOP.
7. Meanwhile, combine all the sauce ingredients together in a bowl.
8. Remove the shrimp when the cooking time is over.

Nutrition Info:

- (Per serving) Calories 415 | Fat 15g | Sodium 1875mg | Carbs 28g | Fiber 1g | Sugar 5g | Protein 38g

Glazed Scallops

Servings: 6

Cooking Time: 13 Minutes.

Ingredients:

- 12 scallops
- 3 tablespoons olive oil
- Black pepper and salt to taste

Directions:

1. Rub the scallops with olive oil, black pepper, and salt.
2. Divide the scallops in the two crisper plates.
3. Return the crisper plate to the Ninja Foodi Dual Zone Air Fryer.
4. Choose the Air Fry mode for Zone 1 and set the temperature to 390 degrees F and the time to 13 minutes.
5. Select the "MATCH" button to copy the settings for Zone 2.
6. Initiate cooking by pressing the START/STOP button.
7. Flip the scallops once cooked halfway through, and resume cooking.
8. Serve warm.

Nutrition Info:

- (Per serving) Calories 308 | Fat 24g |Sodium 715mg | Carbs 0.8g | Fiber 0.1g | Sugar 0.1g | Protein 21.9g

Broiled Crab Cakes With Hush Puppies

Servings:4

Cooking Time: 15 Minutes

Ingredients:

- FOR THE CRAB CAKES
- 2 large eggs
- 2 tablespoons Dijon mustard
- 2 teaspoons Worcestershire sauce
- 1 teaspoon Old Bay seasoning
- ¼ teaspoon paprika
- ¼ cup cracker crumbs (about 9 crackers)
- 1 pound lump crab meat
- 2 teaspoons vegetable oil
- FOR THE HUSH PUPPIES
- ½ cup all-purpose flour
- 1/3 cup yellow cornmeal
- 3 tablespoons sugar
- ¼ teaspoon kosher salt
- ¼ teaspoon baking powder
- 1 large egg
- ½ cup whole milk
- Nonstick cooking spray

Directions:

1. To prep the crab cakes: In a large bowl, whisk together the eggs, mustard, Worcestershire, Old Bay, and paprika until smooth. Stir in the cracker crumbs until fully incorporated, then fold in the crab meat. Refrigerate the crab mixture for 30 minutes.
2. Divide the crab mixture into 8 equal portions. With damp hands, press each portion gently into a loose patty. Brush both sides of each patty with the oil.

3. To prep the hush puppies: In a large bowl, combine the flour, cornmeal, sugar, salt, and baking powder. Stir in the egg and milk to form a stiff batter.

4. Roll the batter into 8 balls. Spritz each hush puppy with cooking spray.

5. To cook the crab cakes and hush puppies: Install a crisper plate in each of the two baskets. Place the crab cakes in a single layer in the Zone 1 basket and insert the basket in the unit. Line the Zone 2 plate with aluminum foil and spray the foil with cooking spray. Arrange the hush puppies on the foil and insert the basket in the unit.

6. Select Zone 1, select AIR BROIL, set the temperature to 400°F, and set the timer to 15 minutes.

7. Select Zone 2, select AIR FRY, set the temperature to 400°F, and set the timer to 7 minutes. Select SMART FINISH.

8. Press START/PAUSE to begin cooking.

9. When cooking is complete, the crab cakes and hush puppies will be golden brown and cooked through. Serve hot.

Nutrition Info:

- (Per serving) Calories: 403; Total fat: 16g; Saturated fat: 2g; Carbohydrates: 40g; Fiber: 1g; Protein: 27g; Sodium: 872mg

Salmon With Coconut

Servings:2

Cooking Time:15

Ingredients:

- Oil spray, for greasing
- 2 salmon fillets, 6ounces each
- Salt and ground black pepper, to taste
- 1 tablespoon butter, for frying
- 1 tablespoon red curry paste
- 1 cup of coconut cream
- 2 tablespoons fresh cilantro, chopped
- 1 cup of cauliflower florets
- ½ cup Parmesan cheese, hard

Directions:

1. Take a bowl and mix salt, black pepper, butter, red curry paste, coconut cream in a bowl and marinate the salmon in it.

2. Oil sprays the cauliflower florets and then seasons it with salt and freshly ground black pepper.

3. Put the florets in the zone 1 basket.

4. Layer the parchment paper over the zone 2 baskets, and then place the salmon fillet on it.

5. Set the zone 2 basket to AIR FRY mod at 15 minutes for4 00 degrees F

6. Hit the smart finish button to finish it at the same time.

7. Once the time for cooking is over, serve the salmon with cauliflower floret with Parmesan cheese drizzle on top.

Nutrition Info:

- (Per serving) Calories 774 | Fat 59g| Sodium 1223mg Carbs 12.2g | Fiber 3.9g | Sugar5.9 g | Protein53.5 g

Spicy Salmon Fillets

Servings: 6

Cooking Time: 8 Minutes

Ingredients:

- 900g salmon fillets
- ¾ tsp ground cumin
- 1 tbsp brown sugar
- 2 tbsp steak seasoning
- ¼ tsp cayenne pepper
- ½ tsp ground coriander

Directions:

1. Mix ground cumin, coriander, steak seasoning, brown sugar, and cayenne in a small bowl.

2. Rub salmon fillets with spice mixture.

3. Insert a crisper plate in the Ninja Foodi air fryer baskets.

4. Place the salmon fillets in both baskets.

5. Select zone 1, then select "bake" mode and set the temperature to 360 degrees F for 10 minutes. Press "match" to match zone 2 settings to zone 1. Press "start/stop" to begin.

Nutrition Info:

- (Per serving) Calories 207 | Fat 9.4g |Sodium 68mg | Carbs 1.6g | Fiber 0.1g | Sugar 1.5g | Protein 29.4g

Salmon Nuggets

Servings: 4

Cooking Time: 15 Minutes.

Ingredients:

- ⅓ cup maple syrup
- ¼ teaspoon dried chipotle pepper
- 1 pinch sea salt
- 1 ½ cups croutons
- 1 large egg
- 1 (1 pound) skinless salmon fillet, cut into 1 ½-inch chunk
- cooking spray

Directions:

1. Mix chipotle powder, maple syrup, and salt in a saucepan and cook on a simmer for 5 minutes.

2. Crush the croutons in a food processor and transfer to a bowl.

3. Beat egg in another shallow bowl.

4. Season the salmon chunks with sea salt.

5. Dip the salmon in the egg, then coat with breadcrumbs.

6. Divide the coated salmon chunks in the two crisper plates.

7. Return the crisper plate to the Ninja Foodi Dual Zone Air Fryer.

8. Select the Air Fry mode for Zone 1 and set the temperature to 390 degrees F and the time to 10 minutes.

9. Press the "MATCH" button to copy the settings for Zone 2.

10. Initiate cooking by pressing the START/STOP button.

11. Flip the chunks once cooked halfway through, then resume cooking.

12. Pour the maple syrup on top and serve warm.

Nutrition Info:
- (Per serving) Calories 275 | Fat 1.4g |Sodium 582mg | Carbs 31.5g | Fiber 1.1g | Sugar 0.1g | Protein 29.8g

Crusted Shrimp

Servings: 4
Cooking Time: 13 Minutes.
Ingredients:
- 1 lb. shrimp
- ½ cup flour, all-purpose
- 1 teaspoon salt
- ½ teaspoon baking powder
- ⅔ cup water
- 2 cups coconut shred
- ½ cup bread crumbs

Directions:
1. In a small bowl, whisk together flour, salt, water, and baking powder. Set aside for 5 minutes.

2. In another shallow bowl, toss bread crumbs with coconut shreds together.

3. Dredge shrimp in liquid, then coat in coconut mixture, making sure it's totally covered.

4. Repeat until all shrimp are coated.

5. Spread half of the shrimp in each crisper plate and spray them with cooking oil.

6. Return the crisper plates to the Ninja Foodi Dual Zone Air Fryer.

7. Choose the Air Fry mode for Zone 1 and set the temperature to 390 degrees F and the time to 13 minutes.

8. Select the "MATCH" button to copy the settings for Zone 2.

9. Initiate cooking by pressing the START/STOP button.

10. Shake the baskets once cooked halfway, then resume cooking.

11. Serve with your favorite dip.

Nutrition Info:
- (Per serving) Calories 297 | Fat 1g |Sodium 291mg | Carbs 35g | Fiber 1g | Sugar 9g | Protein 29g

Herb Tuna Patties

Servings: 10
Cooking Time: 12 Minutes
Ingredients:
- 2 eggs
- 425g can tuna, drained & diced
- ½ tsp garlic powder
- ½ small onion, minced
- 1 celery stalk, chopped
- 42g parmesan cheese, grated
- 50g breadcrumbs
- ½ tsp dried oregano
- ½ tsp dried basil
- ½ tsp dried thyme
- 15ml lemon juice
- 1 lemon zest
- Pepper
- Salt

Directions:
1. In a bowl, mix tuna with remaining ingredients until well combined.

2. Insert a crisper plate in the Ninja Foodi air fryer baskets.

3. Make patties from the tuna mixture and place them in both baskets.

4. Select zone 1, then select "bake" mode and set the temperature to 380 degrees F for 12 minutes. Press "match" to match zone 2 settings to zone 1. Press "start/stop" to begin. Turn halfway through.

Nutrition Info:
- (Per serving) Calories 86 | Fat 1.5g |Sodium 90mg | Carbs 4.5g | Fiber 0.4g | Sugar 0.6g | Protein 12.8g

Beer Battered Fish Fillet

Servings:2
Cooking Time:14
Ingredients:
- 1 cup all-purpose flour
- 4 tablespoons cornstarch
- 1 teaspoon baking soda
- 8 ounces beer
- 2 egg beaten
- ½ cup all-purpose flour
- 1 teaspoon smoked paprika
- 1 teaspoon salt
- 1/4 teaspoon freshly ground black pepper
- ¼ teaspoon of cayenne pepper
- 2 cod fillets, 1½-inches thick, cut into 4 pieces
- Oil spray, for greasing

Directions:
1. Take a large bowl and combine flour, baking soda, corn starch, and salt

2. In a separate bowl beat eggs along with the beer.

3. In a shallow dish mix paprika, salt, pepper, and cayenne pepper.

4. Dry the codfish fillets with a paper towel.

5. Dip the fish into the eggs and coat it with seasoned flour.

6. Then dip it in the seasoning.
7. Grease the fillet with oil spray.
8. Divide the fillet between both zones.
9. Set zone 1 to AIR FRY mode at 400 degrees F for 14 minutes.
10. Select MACTH button for zone 2 basket.
11. Press start and let the AIR fry do its magic.
12. Once cooking is done, serve the fish.
13. Enjoy it hot.

Nutrition Info:

- (Per serving) Calories 1691| Fat 6.1g| Sodium 3976mg | Carbs105.1 g | Fiber 3.4g | Sugar15.6 g | Protein 270g

Scallops With Greens

Servings: 8
Cooking Time: 13 Minutes.

Ingredients:

- ¾ cup heavy whipping cream
- 1 tablespoon tomato paste
- 1 tablespoon chopped fresh basil
- 1 teaspoon garlic, minced
- ½ teaspoons salt
- ½ teaspoons pepper
- 12 ounces frozen spinach thawed
- 8 jumbo sea scallops
- Vegetable oil to spray

Directions:

1. Season the scallops with vegetable oil, salt, and pepper in a bowl
2. Mix cream with spinach, basil, garlic, salt, pepper, and tomato paste in a bowl.
3. Pour this mixture over the scallops and mix gently.
4. Divide the scallops in the Air Fryers Baskets without using the crisper plate.
5. Return the crisper plate to the Ninja Foodi Dual Zone Air Fryer.
6. Choose the Air Fry mode for Zone 1 and set the temperature to 390 degrees F and the time to 13 minutes.
7. Select the "MATCH" button to copy the settings for Zone 2.
8. Initiate cooking by pressing the START/STOP button.
9. Serve right away

Nutrition Info:

- (Per serving) Calories 266 | Fat 6.3g |Sodium 193mg | Carbs 39.1g | Fiber 7.2g | Sugar 5.2g | Protein 14.8g

Smoked Salmon

Servings:4
Cooking Time:12

Ingredients:

- 2 pounds of salmon fillets, smoked

- 6 ounces cream cheese
- 4 tablespoons mayonnaise
- 2 teaspoons of chives, fresh
- 1 teaspoon of lemon zest
- Salt and freshly ground black pepper, to taste
- 2 tablespoons of butter

Directions:

1. Cut the salmon into very small and uniform bite-size pieces.
2. Mix cream cheese, chives, mayonnaise, black pepper, and lemon zest, in a small mixing bowl.
3. Let it sit aside for further use.
4. Coat the salmon pieces with salt and butter.
5. Divide the bite-size pieces into both zones of the air fryer.
6. Set it on AIRFRY mode at 400 degrees F for 12 minutes.
7. Select MATCH for zone 2 basket.
8. Hit start, so the cooking start.
9. Once the salmon is done, top it with a bowl creamy mixture and serve.
10. Enjoy hot.

Nutrition Info:

- (Per serving) Calories 557| Fat 15.7 g| Sodium 371mg | Carbs 4.8 g | Fiber 0g | Sugar 1.1g | Protein 48 g

Crumb-topped Sole

Servings: 4
Cooking Time: 7 Minutes

Ingredients:

- 3 tablespoons mayonnaise
- 3 tablespoons Parmesan cheese, grated
- 2 teaspoons mustard seeds
- ¼ teaspoon black pepper
- 4 (170g) sole fillets
- 1 cup soft bread crumbs
- 1 green onion, chopped
- ½ teaspoon ground mustard
- 2 teaspoons butter, melted
- Cooking spray

Directions:

1. Mix mayonnaise with black pepper, mustard seeds, and 2 tablespoons cheese in a bowl.
2. Place 2 sole fillets in each air fryer basket and top them with mayo mixture.
3. Mix breadcrumbs with rest of the ingredients in a bowl.
4. Drizzle this mixture over the sole fillets.
5. Return the air fryer basket 1 to Zone 1, and basket 2 to Zone 2 of the Ninja Foodi 2-Basket Air Fryer.
6. Choose the "Air Fry" mode for Zone 1 and set the temperature to 375 degrees F and 7 minutes of cooking time.

7. Select the "MATCH COOK" option to copy the settings for Zone 2.

8. Initiate cooking by pressing the START/PAUSE BUTTON.

9. Serve warm.

Nutrition Info:

- (Per serving) Calories 308 | Fat 24g |Sodium 715mg | Carbs 0.8g | Fiber 0.1g | Sugar 0.1g | Protein 21.9g

Broiled Teriyaki Salmon With Eggplant In Stir-fry Sauce

Servings:4

Cooking Time: 25 Minutes

Ingredients:

- FOR THE TERIYAKI SALMON
- 4 salmon fillets (6 ounces each)
- ½ cup teriyaki sauce
- 3 scallions, sliced
- FOR THE EGGPLANT
- ¼ cup reduced-sodium soy sauce
- ¼ cup packed light brown sugar
- 1 tablespoon minced fresh ginger
- 1 tablespoon minced garlic
- 2 teaspoons sesame oil
- ¼ teaspoon red pepper flakes
- 1 eggplant, peeled and cut into bite-size cubes
- Nonstick cooking spray

Directions:

1. To prep the teriyaki salmon: Brush the top of each salmon fillet with the teriyaki sauce.

2. To prep the eggplant: In a small bowl, whisk together the soy sauce, brown sugar, ginger, garlic, sesame oil, and red pepper flakes. Set the stir-fry sauce aside.

3. Spritz the eggplant cubes with cooking spray.

4. To cook the salmon and eggplant: Install a crisper plate in each of the two baskets. Place the salmon in a single layer in the Zone 1 basket and insert the basket in the unit. Place the eggplant in the Zone 2 basket and insert the basket in the unit.

5. Select Zone 1, select AIR BROIL, set the temperature to 450°F, and set the time to 8 minutes.

6. Select Zone 2, select AIR FRY, set the temperature to 390°F, and set the time to 25 minutes. Select SMART FINISH.

7. Press START/PAUSE to begin cooking.

8. When the Zone 2 timer reads 5 minutes, press START/PAUSE. Remove the basket and pour the stir-fry sauce evenly over the eggplant. Shake or stir to coat the eggplant cubes in the sauce. Reinsert the basket and press START/PAUSE to resume cooking.

9. When cooking is complete, the salmon should be cooked to your liking and the eggplant tender and slightly caramelized. Serve hot.

Nutrition Info:

- (Per serving) Calories: 499; Total fat: 22g; Saturated fat: 2g; Carbohydrates: 36g; Fiber: 3.5g; Protein: 42g; Sodium: 1,024mg

Parmesan-crusted Fish Sticks With Baked Macaroni And Cheese

Servings:4

Cooking Time: 25 Minutes

Ingredients:

- FOR THE FISH STICKS
- 1 pound cod or haddock fillets
- ½ cup all-purpose flour
- 2 large eggs
- ¼ teaspoon kosher salt
- ¼ teaspoon freshly ground black pepper
- ¾ cup panko bread crumbs
- ¼ cup grated Parmesan cheese
- Nonstick cooking spray
- FOR THE MACARONI AND CHEESE
- 1½ cups elbow macaroni
- 1 cup whole milk
- ½ cup heavy (whipping) cream
- 8 ounces shredded Colby-Jack cheese
- 4 ounces cream cheese, at room temperature
- 1 teaspoon Dijon mustard
- ½ teaspoon kosher salt
- ½ teaspoon freshly ground black pepper

Directions:

1. To prep the fish sticks: Cut the fish into sticks about 3 inches long and ¾ inch wide.

2. Set up a breading station with three small shallow bowls. Place the flour in the first bowl. In the second bowl, whisk the eggs and season with the salt and black pepper. Combine the panko and Parmesan in the third bowl.

3. Bread the fish sticks in this order: First, dip them into the flour, coating all sides. Then, dip into the beaten egg. Finally, coat them in the panko mixture, gently pressing the bread crumbs into the fish. Spritz each fish stick all over with cooking spray.

4. To prep the macaroni and cheese: Place the macaroni in the Zone 2 basket. Add the milk, cream, Colby-Jack, cream cheese, mustard, salt, and black pepper. Stir well to combine, ensuring the pasta is completely submerged in the liquid.

5. To cook the fish sticks and macaroni and cheese: Install a crisper plate in the Zone 1 basket. Arrange the fish sticks in a single layer in the basket (use a rack or cook in batches if

necessary) and insert the basket in the unit. Insert the Zone 2 basket in the unit.

6. Select Zone 1, select AIR FRY, set the temperature to 390°F, and set the timer to 18 minutes.

7. Select Zone 2, select BAKE, set the temperature to 360°F, and set the timer to 25 minutes. Select SMART FINISH.

8. Press START/PAUSE to begin cooking.

9. When the Zone 1 timer reads 3 minutes, press START/PAUSE. Remove the basket and use silicone-tipped tongs to gently flip over the fish sticks. Reinsert the basket and press START/PAUSE to resume cooking.

10. When cooking is complete, the fish sticks should be crisp and the macaroni tender.

11. Stir the macaroni and cheese and let stand for 5 minutes before serving. The sauce will thicken as it cools.

Nutrition Info:

- (Per serving) Calories: 903; Total fat: 51g; Saturated fat: 25g; Carbohydrates: 60g; Fiber: 2.5g; Protein: 48g; Sodium: 844mg

Garlic Shrimp With Pasta Alfredo

Servings:4
Cooking Time: 40 Minutes
Ingredients:

- FOR THE GARLIC SHRIMP
- 1 pound peeled small shrimp, thawed if frozen
- 1 tablespoon olive oil
- 1 tablespoon minced garlic
- ¼ teaspoon sea salt
- ¼ cup chopped fresh parsley
- FOR THE PASTA ALFREDO
- 8 ounces no-boil lasagna noodles
- 2 cups whole milk
- ¼ cup heavy (whipping) cream
- 2 tablespoons unsalted butter, cut into small pieces
- 1 tablespoon minced garlic
- ½ teaspoon kosher salt
- ¼ teaspoon freshly ground black pepper
- ½ cup grated Parmesan cheese

Directions:

1. To prep the garlic shrimp: In a large bowl, combine the shrimp, oil, garlic, and salt.

2. To prep the pasta alfredo: Break the lasagna noodles into 2-inch pieces. Add the milk to the Zone 2 basket, then add the noodles, cream, butter, garlic, salt, and black pepper. Stir well and ensure the pasta is fully submerged in the liquid.

3. To cook the shrimp and pasta: Install a crisper plate in the Zone 1 basket. Place the shrimp in the basket and insert the basket in the unit. Insert the Zone 2 basket in the unit.

4. Select Zone 1, select AIR FRY, set the temperature to 390°F, and set the timer to 13 minutes.

5. Select Zone 2, select BAKE, set the temperature to 360°F, and set the timer to 40 minutes. Select SMART FINISH.

6. Press START/PAUSE to begin cooking.

7. When the Zone 2 timer reads 20 minutes, press START/PAUSE. Remove the basket and stir the pasta. Reinsert the basket and press START/PAUSE to resume cooking.

8. When cooking is complete, the shrimp will be cooked through and the pasta tender.

9. Transfer the pasta to a serving dish and stir in the Parmesan. Top with the shrimp and parsley.

Nutrition Info:

- (Per serving) Calories: 542; Total fat: 23g; Saturated fat: 11g; Carbohydrates: 52g; Fiber: 2g; Protein: 34g; Sodium: 643mg

Salmon With Fennel Salad

Servings: 4
Cooking Time: 17 Minutes.
Ingredients:

- 2 teaspoons fresh parsley, chopped
- 1 teaspoon fresh thyme, chopped
- 1 teaspoon salt
- 4 (6-oz) skinless center-cut salmon fillets
- 2 tablespoons olive oil
- 4 cups fennel, sliced
- ⅔ cup Greek yogurt
- 1 garlic clove, grated
- 2 tablespoons orange juice
- 1 teaspoon lemon juice
- 2 tablespoons fresh dill, chopped

Directions:

1. Preheat your Ninja Foodi Dual Zone Air Fryer to 200 degrees F.

2. Mix ½ teaspoon of salt, thyme, and parsley in a small bowl.

3. Brush the salmon with oil first, then rub liberally rub the herb mixture.

4. Place 2 salmon fillets in each of the crisper plate.

5. Return the crisper plate to the Ninja Foodi Dual Zone Air Fryer.

6. Choose the Air Fry mode for Zone 1 and set the temperature to 390 degrees F and the time to 17 minutes.

7. Select the "MATCH" button to copy the settings for Zone 2.

8. Initiate cooking by pressing the START/STOP button.

9. Meanwhile, mix fennel with garlic, yogurt, lemon juice, orange juice, remaining salt, and dill in a mixing bowl.

10. Serve the air fried salmon fillets with fennel salad.

11. Enjoy.

Nutrition Info:

- (Per serving) Calories 305 | Fat 15g |Sodium 482mg | Carbs 17g | Fiber 3g | Sugar 2g | Protein 35g

Fried Tilapia

Servings: 4

Cooking Time: 20 Minutes

Ingredients:

- 4 fresh tilapia fillets, approximately 6 ounces each
- 2 teaspoons olive oil
- 2 teaspoons chopped fresh chives
- 2 teaspoons chopped fresh parsley
- 1 teaspoon minced garlic
- Freshly ground pepper, to taste
- Salt to taste

Directions:

1. Pat the tilapia fillets dry with a paper towel.
2. Stir together the olive oil, chives, parsley, garlic, salt, and pepper in a small bowl.
3. Brush the mixture over the top of the tilapia fillets.
4. Place a crisper plate in each drawer. Add the fillets in a single layer to each drawer. Insert the drawers into the unit.
5. Select zone 1, then AIR FRY, then set the temperature to 360 degrees F/ 180 degrees C with a 20-minute timer. To match zone 2 settings to zone 1, choose MATCH. To begin, select START/STOP.
6. Remove the tilapia fillets from the drawers after the timer has finished.

Nutrition Info:

- (Per serving) Calories 140 | Fat 5.7g | Sodium 125mg | Carbs 1.5g | Fiber 0.4g | Sugar 0g | Protein 21.7g

Keto Baked Salmon With Pesto

Servings:2

Cooking Time:18

Ingredients:

- 4 salmon fillets, 2 inches thick
- 2 ounces green pesto
- Salt and black pepper
- ½ tablespoon of canola oil, for greasing
- 1-1/2 cup mayonnaise
- 2 tablespoons Greek yogurt
- Salt and black pepper, to taste

Directions:

1. Rub the salmon with pesto, salt, oil, and black pepper.
2. In a small bowl, whisk together all the green sauce ingredients.
3. Divide the fish fillets between both the baskets.
4. Set zone 1 to air fry mode for 18 minutes at 390 degrees F.
5. Select MATCH button for Zone 2 basket
6. Once the cooking is done, serve it with green sauce drizzle.
7. Enjoy.

Nutrition Info:

- (Per serving) Calories 1165 | Fat80.7 g| Sodium 1087 mg | Carbs 33.1g | Fiber 0.5g | Sugar11.5 g | Protein 80.6g

Chili Lime Tilapia

Servings: 4

Cooking Time: 10 Minutes

Ingredients:

- 340g tilapia fillets
- 2 teaspoons chili powder
- 1 teaspoon cumin
- 1 teaspoon garlic powder
- ½ teaspoon oregano
- ½ teaspoon sea salt
- ¼ teaspoon black pepper
- Lime zest from 1 lime
- Juice of ½ lime

Directions:

1. Mix chili powder and other spices with lime juice and zest in a bowl.
2. Rub this spice mixture over the tilapia fillets.
3. Place two fillets in each air basket.
4. Return the air fryer basket to the Ninja Foodi 2 Baskets Air Fryer.
5. Choose the "Air Fry" mode for Zone 1 at 400 degrees F and 10 minutes of cooking time.
6. Select the "MATCH COOK" option to copy the settings for Zone 2.
7. Initiate cooking by pressing the START/PAUSE BUTTON.
8. Flip the tilapia fillets once cooked halfway through.
9. Serve warm.

Nutrition Info:

- (Per serving) Calories 275 | Fat 1.4g |Sodium 582mg | Carbs 31.5g | Fiber 1.1g | Sugar 0.1g | Protein 29.8g

Savory Salmon Fillets

Servings: 4

Cooking Time: 17 Minutes.

Ingredients:

- 4 (6-oz) salmon fillets
- Salt, to taste
- Black pepper, to taste
- 4 teaspoons olive oil
- 4 tablespoons wholegrain mustard
- 2 tablespoons packed brown sugar
- 2 garlic cloves, minced
- 1 teaspoon thyme leaves

Directions:

1. Rub the salmon with salt and black pepper first.

2. Whisk oil with sugar, thyme, garlic, and mustard in a small bowl.

3. Place two salmon fillets in each of the crisper plate and brush the thyme mixture on top of each fillet.

4. Return the crisper plates to the Ninja Foodi Dual Zone Air Fryer.

5. Choose the Air Fry mode for Zone 1 and set the temperature to 390 degrees F and the time to 17 minutes.

6. Select the "MATCH" button to copy the settings for Zone 2.

7. Initiate cooking by pressing the START/STOP button.

8. Serve warm and fresh.

Nutrition Info:

- (Per serving) Calories 336 | Fat 6g |Sodium 181mg | Carbs 1.3g | Fiber 0.2g | Sugar 0.4g | Protein 69.2g

Honey Sriracha Mahi Mahi

Servings: 4

Cooking Time: 7 Minutes

Ingredients:

- 3 pounds mahi-mahi
- 6 tablespoons honey
- 4 tablespoons sriracha
- Salt, to taste
- Cooking spray

Directions:

1. In a small bowl, mix the sriracha sauce and honey. Mix well.

2. Season the fish with salt and pour the honey mixture over it. Let it sit at room temperature for 20 minutes.

3. Place a crisper plate in each drawer. Put the fish in a single layer in each. Insert the drawers into the unit.

4. Select zone 1, then AIR FRY, then set the temperature to 400 degrees F/ 200 degrees C with a 7-minute timer. To match zone 2 settings to zone 1, choose MATCH. To begin, select START/STOP.

5. Remove the fish from the drawers after the timer has finished.

Nutrition Info:

- (Per serving) Calories 581 | Fat 22g | Sodium 495mg | Carbs 26g | Fiber 4g | Sugar 26g | Protein 68g

Fried Lobster Tails

Servings: 4

Cooking Time: 18 Minutes.

Ingredients:

- 4 (4-oz) lobster tails
- 8 tablespoons butter, melted
- 2 teaspoons lemon zest
- 2 garlic cloves, grated
- Salt and black pepper, ground to taste

- 2 teaspoons fresh parsley, chopped
- 4 wedges lemon

Directions:

1. Spread the lobster tails into Butterfly, slit the top to expose the lobster meat while keeping the tail intact.

2. Place two lobster tails in each of the crisper plate with their lobster meat facing up.

3. Mix melted butter with lemon zest and garlic in a bowl.

4. Brush the butter mixture on top of the lobster tails.

5. And drizzle salt and black pepper on top.

6. Return the crisper plate to the Ninja Foodi Dual Zone Air Fryer.

7. Choose the Air Fry mode for Zone 1 and set the temperature to 390 degrees F and the time to 18 minutes.

8. Select the "MATCH" button to copy the settings for Zone 2.

9. Initiate cooking by pressing the START/STOP button.

10. Garnish with parsley and lemon wedges.

11. Serve warm.

Nutrition Info:

- (Per serving) Calories 257 | Fat 10.4g |Sodium 431mg | Carbs 20g | Fiber 0g | Sugar 1.6g | Protein 21g

Seafood Shrimp Omelet

Servings:2

Cooking Time:15

Ingredients:

- 6 large shrimp, shells removed and chopped
- 6 eggs, beaten
- ½ tablespoon of butter, melted
- 2 tablespoons green onions, sliced
- 1/3 cup of mushrooms, chopped
- 1 pinch paprika
- Salt and black pepper, to taste
- Oil spray, for greasing

Directions:

1. In a large bowl whisk the eggs and add chopped shrimp, butter, green onions, mushrooms, paprika, salt, and black pepper.

2. Take two cake pans that fit inside the air fryer and grease them with oil spray.

3. Pour the egg mixture between the cake pans and place it in two baskets of the air fryer.

4. Turn on the BAKE function of zone 1, and let it cook for 15 minutes at 320 degrees F.

5. Select the MATCH button to match the cooking time for the zone 2 basket.

6. Once the cooking cycle completes, take out, and serve hot.

Nutrition Info:

- (Per serving) Calories 300 | Fat 17.5g| Sodium 368mg | Carbs 2.9g | Fiber 0.3g | Sugar1.4 g | Protein32.2 g

Codfish With Herb Vinaigrette

Servings:2
Cooking Time:16
Ingredients:
- Vinaigrette Ingredients:
- 1/2 cup parsley leaves
- 1 cup basil leaves
- ½ cup mint leaves
- 2 tablespoons thyme leaves
- 1/4 teaspoon red pepper flakes
- 2 cloves of garlic
- 4 tablespoons of red wine vinegar
- ¼ cup of olive oil
- Salt, to taste
- Other Ingredients:
- 1.5 pounds fish fillets, cod fish
- 2 tablespoons olive oil
- Salt and black pepper, to taste
- 1 teaspoon of paprika
- 1teasbpoon of Italian seasoning

Directions:
1. Blend the entire vinaigrette ingredient in a high-speed blender and pulse into a smooth paste.
2. Set aside for drizzling overcooked fish.
3. Rub the fillets with salt, black pepper, paprika, Italian seasoning, and olive oil.
4. Divide it between two baskets of the air fryer.

5. Set the zone 1 to 16 minutes at 390 degrees F, at AIR FRY mode.
6. Press the MATCH button for the second basket.
7. Once done, serve the fillets with the drizzle of blended vinaigrette

Nutrition Info:
- (Per serving) Calories 1219| Fat 81.8g| Sodium 1906mg | Carbs64.4 g | Fiber5.5 g | Sugar 0.4g | Protein 52.1g

Frozen Breaded Fish Fillet

Servings:2
Cooking Time:12
Ingredients:
- 4 Frozen Breaded Fish Fillet
- Oil spray, for greasing
- 1 cup mayonnaise

Directions:
1. Take the frozen fish fillets out of the bag and place them in both baskets of the air fryer.
2. Lightly grease it with oil spray.
3. Set the Zone 1 basket to 380 degrees F fo12 minutes.
4. Select the MATCH button for the zone 2 basket.
5. hit the start button to start cooking.
6. Once the cooking is done, serve the fish hot with mayonnaise.

Nutrition Info:
- (Per serving) Calories 921| Fat 61.5g| Sodium 1575mg | Carbs 69g | Fiber 2g | Sugar 9.5g | Protein 29.1g

Vegetables And Sides Recipes

Buffalo Seitan With Crispy Zucchini Noodles

Servings:4
Cooking Time: 12 Minutes
Ingredients:

- FOR THE BUFFALO SEITAN
- 1 (8-ounce) package precooked seitan strips
- 1 teaspoon garlic powder, divided
- ½ teaspoon onion powder
- ¼ teaspoon smoked paprika
- ¼ cup Louisiana-style hot sauce
- 2 tablespoons vegetable oil
- 1 tablespoon tomato paste
- ¼ teaspoon freshly ground black pepper
- FOR THE ZUCCHINI NOODLES
- 3 large egg whites
- 1¼ cups all-purpose flour
- 1 teaspoon kosher salt, divided
- 12 ounces seltzer water or club soda
- 5 ounces zucchini noodles
- Nonstick cooking spray

Directions:

1. To prep the Buffalo seitan: Season the seitan strips with ½ teaspoon of garlic powder, the onion powder, and smoked paprika.
2. In a large bowl, whisk together the hot sauce, oil, tomato paste, remaining ½ teaspoon of garlic powder, and the black pepper. Set the bowl of Buffalo sauce aside.
3. To prep the zucchini noodles: In a medium bowl, use a handheld mixer to beat the egg whites until stiff peaks form.
4. In a large bowl, combine the flour and ½ teaspoon of salt. Mix in the seltzer to form a thin batter. Fold in the beaten egg whites.
5. Add the zucchini to the batter and gently mix to coat.
6. To cook the seitan and zucchini noodles: Install a crisper plate in each of the two baskets. Place the seitan in the Zone 1 basket and insert the basket in the unit. Lift the noodles from the batter one at a time, letting the excess drip off, and place them in the Zone 2 basket. Insert the basket in the unit.
7. Select Zone 1, select BAKE, set the temperature to 370°F, and set the timer to 12 minutes.
8. Select Zone 2, select AIR FRY, set the temperature to 400°F, and set the timer to 12 minutes. Select SMART FINISH.
9. Press START/PAUSE to begin cooking.
10. When the Zone 1 timer reads 2 minutes, press START/PAUSE. Remove the basket and transfer the seitan to the bowl of Buffalo sauce. Turn to coat, then return the seitan to the basket. Reinsert the basket and press START/PAUSE to resume cooking.
11. When cooking is complete, the seitan should be warmed through and the zucchini noodles crisp and light golden brown.
12. Sprinkle the zucchini noodles with the remaining ½ teaspoon of salt. If desired, drizzle extra Buffalo sauce over the seitan. Serve hot.

Nutrition Info:

- (Per serving) Calories: 252; Total fat: 15g; Saturated fat: 1g; Carbohydrates: 22g; Fiber: 1.5g; Protein: 13g; Sodium: 740mg

Mixed Air Fry Veggies

Servings:4
Cooking Time:25
Ingredients:

- 2 cups of carrots, cubed
- 2 cups of potatoes, cubed
- 2 cups of shallots, cubed
- 2 cups zucchini, diced
- 2 cups yellow squash, cubed
- Salt and black pepper, to taste
- 1 tablespoon of Italian seasoning
- 2 tablespoons of ranch seasoning
- 4 tablespoons of olive oil

Directions:

1. Take a large bowl and add all the veggies to it.
2. Season the veggies with salt, pepper, Italian seasoning, ranch seasoning, and olive oil
3. Toss all the ingredients well.
4. Now divide this between two baskets of the air fryer.
5. Set zone 1 basket to AIRFRY mode at 360 degrees F for 25 minutes.
6. Select the Match button for the zone 2 basket.
7. Once it is cooked and done, serve, and enjoy.

Nutrition Info:

- (Per serving) Calories 275| Fat 15.3g| Sodium129 mg | Carbs 33g | Fiber3.8 g | Sugar5 g | Protein 4.4g

Fresh Mix Veggies In Air Fryer

Servings:4

Cooking Time:12

Ingredients:

- 1 cup cauliflower florets
- 1 cup of carrots, peeled chopped
- 1 cup broccoli florets
- 2 tablespoons of avocado oil
- Salt, to taste
- ½ teaspoon of chili powder
- ½ teaspoon of garlic powder
- ½ teaspoon of herbs de Provence
- 1 cup parmesan cheese

Directions:

1. Take a bowl, and add all the veggies to it.
2. Toss and then season the veggies with salt, chili powder, garlic powder, and herbs de Provence.
3. Toss it all well and then drizzle avocado oil.
4. Make sure the ingredients are coated well.
5. Now distribute the veggies among both baskets of the air fryer.
6. Turn on the start button and set it to AIR FRY mode at 390 degrees for 10-12 minutes.
7. For the zone 2 basket setting, press the MATCH button.
8. After 8 minutes of cooking, select the pause button and then take out the baskets and sprinkle Parmesan cheese on top of the veggies.
9. Then let the cooking cycle complete for the next 3-4 minutes.
10. Once done, serve.

Nutrition Info:

- (Per serving) Calories161 | Fat 9.3g| Sodium434 mg | Carbs 7.7g | Fiber 2.4g | Sugar 2.5g | Protein 13.9

Air Fryer Vegetables

Servings: 2

Cooking Time: 15 Minutes

Ingredients:

- 1 courgette, diced
- 2 capsicums, diced
- 1 head broccoli, diced
- 1 red onion, diced
- Marinade
- 1 teaspoon smoked paprika
- 1 teaspoon garlic granules
- 1 teaspoon Herb de Provence
- Salt and black pepper, to taste
- 1½ tablespoon olive oil
- 2 tablespoons lemon juice

Directions:

1. Toss the veggies with the rest of the marinade ingredients in a bowl.
2. Spread the veggies in the air fryer baskets.
3. Return the air fryer basket 1 to Zone 1, and basket 2 to Zone 2 of the Ninja Foodi 2-Basket Air Fryer.
4. Choose the "Air Fry" mode for Zone 1 at 400 degrees F and 15 minutes of cooking time.
5. Select the "MATCH COOK" option to copy the settings for Zone 2.
6. Initiate cooking by pressing the START/PAUSE BUTTON.
7. Toss the veggies once cooked half way through.
8. Serve warm.

Nutrition Info:

- (Per serving) Calories 166 | Fat 3.2g |Sodium 437mg | Carbs 28.8g | Fiber 1.8g | Sugar 2.7g | Protein 5.8g

Acorn Squash Slices

Servings: 6

Cooking Time: 10 Minutes

Ingredients:

- 2 medium acorn squashes
- ⅔ cup packed brown sugar
- ½ cup butter, melted

Directions:

1. Cut the squash in half, remove the seeds and slice into ½ inch slices.
2. Place the squash slices in the air fryer baskets.
3. Drizzle brown sugar and butter over the squash slices.
4. Return the air fryer basket 1 to Zone 1, and basket 2 to Zone 2 of the Ninja Foodi 2-Basket Air Fryer.
5. Choose the "Air Fry" mode for Zone 1 and set the temperature to 350 degrees F and 10 minutes of cooking time.
6. Select the "MATCH COOK" option to copy the settings for Zone 2.
7. Initiate cooking by pressing the START/PAUSE BUTTON.
8. Flip the squash once cooked halfway through.
9. Serve.

Nutrition Info:

- (Per serving) Calories 206 | Fat 3.4g |Sodium 174mg | Carbs 35g | Fiber 9.4g | Sugar 5.9g | Protein 10.6g

Rosemary Asparagus & Potatoes

Servings: 6
Cooking Time: 30 Minutes
Ingredients:

- 125g asparagus, trimmed & cut into pieces
- 2 tsp garlic powder
- 2 tbsp rosemary, chopped
- 30ml olive oil
- 679g baby potatoes, quartered
- ½ tsp red pepper flakes
- Pepper
- Salt

Directions:

1. Insert a crisper plate in the Ninja Foodi air fryer baskets.
2. Toss potatoes with 1 tablespoon of oil, pepper, and salt in a bowl until well coated.
3. Add potatoes into in zone 1 basket.
4. Toss asparagus with remaining oil, red pepper flakes, pepper, garlic powder, and rosemary in a mixing bowl.
5. Add asparagus into the zone 2 basket.
6. Select zone 1, then select "air fry" mode and set the temperature to 390 degrees F for 20 minutes. Select zone 2, then select "air fry" mode and set the temperature to 390 degrees F for 10 minutes. Press "match" mode, then press "start/stop" to begin.

Nutrition Info:

- (Per serving) Calories 121 | Fat 5g |Sodium 40mg | Carbs 17.1g | Fiber 4.2g | Sugar 1g | Protein 4g

Fried Asparagus

Servings: 4
Cooking Time: 6 Minutes
Ingredients:

- ¼ cup mayonnaise
- 4 teaspoons olive oil
- 1½ teaspoons grated lemon zest
- 1 garlic clove, minced
- ½ teaspoon pepper
- ¼ teaspoon seasoned salt
- 1-pound fresh asparagus, trimmed
- 2 tablespoons shredded parmesan cheese
- Lemon wedges (optional)

Directions:

1. In a large bowl, combine the first 6 ingredients.
2. Add the asparagus; toss to coat.
3. Put a crisper plate in both drawers. Put the asparagus in a single layer in each drawer. Top with the parmesan cheese. Place the drawers into the unit.
4. Select zone 1, then AIR FRY, then set the temperature to 375 degrees F/ 190 degrees C with a 6-minute timer. To match

zone 2 settings to zone 1, choose MATCH. To begin, select START/STOP.
5. Remove the asparagus from the drawers after the timer has finished.

Nutrition Info:

- (Per serving) Calories 156 | Fat 15g | Sodium 214mg | Carbs 3g | Fiber 1g | Sugar 1g | Protein 2g

Fried Artichoke Hearts

Servings: 6
Cooking Time: 10 Minutes.
Ingredients:

- 3 cans Quartered Artichokes, drained
- ½ cup mayonnaise
- 1 cup panko breadcrumbs
- ⅓ cup grated Parmesan
- salt and black pepper to taste
- Parsley for garnish

Directions:

1. Mix mayonnaise with salt and black pepper and keep the sauce aside.
2. Spread panko breadcrumbs in a bowl.
3. Coat the artichoke pieces with the breadcrumbs.
4. As you coat the artichokes, place them in the two crisper plates in a single layer, then spray them with cooking oil.
5. Return the crisper plates to the Ninja Foodi Dual Zone Air Fryer.
6. Choose the Air Fry mode for Zone 1 and set the temperature to 375 degrees F and the time to 10 minutes.
7. Select the "MATCH" button to copy the settings for Zone 2.
8. Initiate cooking by pressing the START/STOP button.
9. Flip the artichokes once cooked halfway through, then resume cooking.
10. Serve warm with mayo sauce.

Nutrition Info:

- (Per serving) Calories 193 | Fat 1g |Sodium 395mg | Carbs 38.7g | Fiber 1.6g | Sugar 0.9g | Protein 6.6g

Chickpea Fritters

Servings: 6
Cooking Time: 6 Minutes
Ingredients:

- 237ml plain yogurt
- 2 tablespoons sugar
- 1 tablespoon honey
- ½ teaspoon salt
- ½ teaspoon black pepper
- ½ teaspoon crushed red pepper flakes
- 1 can (28g) chickpeas, drained
- 1 teaspoon ground cumin

- ½ teaspoon salt
- ½ teaspoon garlic powder
- ½ teaspoon ground ginger
- 1 large egg
- ½ teaspoon baking soda
- ½ cup fresh coriander, chopped
- 2 green onions, sliced

Directions:

1. Mash chickpeas with rest of the ingredients in a food processor.
2. Layer the two air fryer baskets with a parchment paper.
3. Drop the batter in the baskets spoon by spoon.
4. Return the air fryer basket 1 to Zone 1, and basket 2 to Zone 2 of the Ninja Foodi 2-Basket Air Fryer.
5. Choose the "Air Fry" mode for Zone 1 at 400 degrees F and 6 minutes of cooking time.
6. Select the "MATCH COOK" option to copy the settings for Zone 2.
7. Initiate cooking by pressing the START/PAUSE BUTTON.
8. Flip the fritters once cooked halfway through.
9. Serve warm.

Nutrition Info:

- (Per serving) Calories 284 | Fat 7.9g |Sodium 704mg | Carbs 38.1g | Fiber 1.9g | Sugar 1.9g | Protein 14.8g

Potatoes & Beans

Servings: 4
Cooking Time: 25 Minutes
Ingredients:

- 453g potatoes, cut into pieces
- 15ml olive oil
- 1 tsp garlic powder
- 160g green beans, trimmed
- Pepper
- Salt

Directions:

1. In a bowl, toss green beans, garlic powder, potatoes, oil, pepper, and salt.
2. Insert a crisper plate in the Ninja Foodi air fryer baskets.
3. Add green beans and potato mixture to both baskets.
4. Select zone 1 then select "air fry" mode and set the temperature to 380 degrees F for 25 minutes. Press "match" to match zone 2 settings to zone 1. Press "start/stop" to begin. Stir halfway through.

Nutrition Info:

- (Per serving) Calories 128 | Fat 3.7g |Sodium 49mg | Carbs 22.4g | Fiber 4.7g | Sugar 2.3g | Protein 3.1g

Pepper Poppers

Servings: 24
Cooking Time: 20 Minutes
Ingredients:

- 8 ounces cream cheese, softened
- ¾ cup shredded cheddar cheese
- ¾ cup shredded Monterey Jack cheese
- 6 bacon strips, cooked and crumbled
- ¼ teaspoon salt
- ¼ teaspoon garlic powder
- ¼ teaspoon chili powder
- ¼ teaspoon smoked paprika
- 1-pound fresh jalapeño peppers, halved lengthwise and deseeded
- ½ cup dry breadcrumbs
- Sour cream, French onion dip, or ranch salad dressing (optional)

Directions:

1. In a large bowl, combine the cheeses, bacon, and seasonings; mix well. Spoon 1½ to 2 tablespoons of the mixture into each pepper half. Roll them in the breadcrumbs.
2. Place a crisper plate in each drawer. Put the prepared peppers in a single layer in each drawer. Insert the drawers into the unit.
3. Select zone 1, then AIR FRY, then set the temperature to 360 degrees F/ 180 degrees C with a 20-minute timer. To match zone 2 settings to zone 1, choose MATCH. To begin, select START/STOP.
4. Remove the peppers from the drawers after the timer has finished.

Nutrition Info:

- (Per serving) Calories 81 | Fat 6g | Sodium 145mg | Carbs 3g | Fiber 4g | Sugar 1g | Protein 3g

Healthy Air Fried Veggies

Servings: 4
Cooking Time: 15 Minutes
Ingredients:

- 52g onion, sliced
- 71g broccoli florets
- 116g radishes, sliced
- 15ml olive oil
- 100g Brussels sprouts, cut in half
- 325g cauliflower florets
- 1 tsp balsamic vinegar
- ½ tsp garlic powder
- Pepper
- Salt

Directions:

1. In a bowl, toss veggies with oil, vinegar, garlic powder, pepper, and salt.
2. Insert a crisper plate in the Ninja Foodi air fryer baskets.
3. Add veggies in both baskets.
4. Select zone 1 then select "air fry" mode and set the temperature to 380 degrees F for 15 minutes. Press "match" to match zone 2 settings to zone 1. Press "start/stop" to begin. Stir halfway through.

Nutrition Info:
- (Per serving) Calories 71 | Fat 3.8g |Sodium 72mg | Carbs 8.8g | Fiber 3.2g | Sugar 3.3g | Protein 2.5g

Brussels Sprouts

Servings:2
Cooking Time:20
Ingredients:
- 2 pounds Brussels sprouts
- 2 tablespoons avocado oil
- Salt and pepper, to taste
- 1 cup pine nuts, roasted

Directions:
1. Trim the bottom of Brussels sprouts.
2. Take a bowl and combine the avocado oil, salt, and black pepper.
3. Toss the Brussels sprouts well.
4. Divide it in both air fryer baskets.
5. For the zone 1 basket use AIR fry mode for 20 minutes at 390 degrees F.
6. Select the MATCH button for the zone 2 basket.
7. Once the Brussels sprouts get crisp and tender, take out and serve.

Nutrition Info:
- (Per serving) Calories 672| Fat 50g| Sodium 115mg | Carbs 51g | Fiber 20.2g | Sugar 12.3g | Protein 25g

Fried Olives

Servings: 6
Cooking Time: 9 Minutes.
Ingredients:
- 2 cups blue cheese stuffed olives, drained
- ½ cup all-purpose flour
- 1 cup panko breadcrumbs
- ½ teaspoon garlic powder
- 1 pinch oregano
- 2 eggs

Directions:
1. Mix flour with oregano and garlic powder in a bowl and beat two eggs in another bowl.
2. Spread panko breadcrumbs in a bowl.
3. Coat all the olives with the flour mixture, dip in the eggs and then coat with the panko breadcrumbs.

4. As you coat the olives, place them in the two crisper plates in a single layer, then spray them with cooking oil.
5. Return the crisper plates to the Ninja Foodi Dual Zone Air Fryer.
6. Choose the Air Fry mode for Zone 1 and set the temperature to 375 degrees F and the time to 9 minutes.
7. Select the "MATCH" button to copy the settings for Zone 2.
8. Initiate cooking by pressing the START/STOP button.
9. Flip the olives once cooked halfway through, then resume cooking.
10. Serve.

Nutrition Info:
- (Per serving) Calories 166 | Fat 3.2g |Sodium 437mg | Carbs 28.8g | Fiber 1.8g | Sugar 2.7g | Protein 5.8g

Fried Patty Pan Squash

Servings: 6
Cooking Time: 15 Minutes
Ingredients:
- 5 cups small pattypan squash, halved
- 1 tablespoon olive oil
- 2 garlic cloves, minced
- ½ teaspoon salt
- ¼ teaspoon dried oregano
- ¼ teaspoon dried thyme
- ¼ teaspoon pepper
- 1 tablespoon minced parsley

Directions:
1. Rub the squash with oil, garlic and the rest of the ingredients.
2. Spread the squash in the air fryer baskets.
3. Return the air fryer basket 1 to Zone 1, and basket 2 to Zone 2 of the Ninja Foodi 2-Basket Air Fryer.
4. Choose the "Air Fry" mode for Zone 1 at 375 degrees F and 15 minutes of cooking time.
5. Select the "MATCH COOK" option to copy the settings for Zone 2.
6. Initiate cooking by pressing the START/PAUSE BUTTON.
7. Flip the squash once cooked halfway through.
8. Garnish with parsley.
9. Serve warm.

Nutrition Info:
- (Per serving) Calories 208 | Fat 5g |Sodium 1205mg | Carbs 34.1g | Fiber 7.8g | Sugar 2.5g | Protein 5.9g

Garlic-rosemary Brussels Sprouts

Servings: 4
Cooking Time: 8 Minutes
Ingredients:
- 3 tablespoons olive oil
- 2 garlic cloves, minced
- ½ teaspoon salt
- ¼ teaspoon black pepper
- 455g Brussels sprouts, halved
- ½ cup panko bread crumbs
- 1-½ teaspoons rosemary, minced

Directions:
1. Toss the Brussels sprouts with crumbs and the rest of the ingredients in a bowl.
2. Divide the sprouts into the Ninja Foodi 2 Baskets Air Fryer baskets.
3. Return the air fryer basket 1 to Zone 1, and basket 2 to Zone 2 of the Ninja Foodi 2-Basket Air Fryer.
4. Choose the "Air Fry" mode for Zone 1 at 350 degrees F and 8 minutes of cooking time.
5. Select the "MATCH COOK" option to copy the settings for Zone 2.
6. Initiate cooking by pressing the START/PAUSE BUTTON.
7. Toss the Brussels sprouts once cooked halfway through.
8. Serve warm.

Nutrition Info:
- (Per serving) Calories 231 | Fat 9g |Sodium 271mg | Carbs 32.8g | Fiber 6.4g | Sugar 7g | Protein 6.3g

Saucy Carrots

Servings: 6
Cooking Time: 25 Minutes.
Ingredients:
- 1 lb. cup carrots, cut into chunks
- 1 tablespoon sesame oil
- ½ tablespoon ginger, minced
- ½ tablespoon soy sauce
- ½ teaspoon garlic, minced
- ½ tablespoon scallions, chopped, for garnish
- ½ teaspoon sesame seeds for garnish

Directions:
1. Toss all the ginger carrots ingredients, except the sesame seeds and scallions, in a suitable bowl.
2. Divide the carrots in the two crisper plates in a single layer.
3. Return the crisper plates to the Ninja Foodi Dual Zone Air Fryer.
4. Choose the Air Fry mode for Zone 1 and set the temperature to 390 degrees F and the time to 25 minutes.
5. Select the "MATCH" button to copy the settings for Zone 2.
6. Initiate cooking by pressing the START/STOP button.
7. Toss the carrots once cooked halfway through.
8. Garnish with sesame seeds and scallions.
9. Serve warm.

Nutrition Info:
- (Per serving) Calories 206 | Fat 3.4g |Sodium 174mg | Carbs 35g | Fiber 9.4g | Sugar 5.9g | Protein 10.6g

Quinoa Patties

Servings: 4
Cooking Time: 32 Minutes.
Ingredients:
- 1 cup quinoa red
- 1½ cups water
- 1 teaspoon salt
- black pepper, ground
- 1½ cups rolled oats
- 3 eggs beaten
- ¼ cup minced white onion
- ½ cup crumbled feta cheese
- ¼ cup chopped fresh chives
- Salt and black pepper, to taste
- Vegetable or canola oil
- 4 hamburger buns
- 4 arugulas
- 4 slices tomato sliced
- Cucumber yogurt dill sauce
- 1 cup cucumber, diced
- 1 cup Greek yogurt
- 2 teaspoons lemon juice
- ¼ teaspoon salt
- Black pepper, ground
- 1 tablespoon chopped fresh dill
- 1 tablespoon olive oil

Directions:
1. Add quinoa to a saucepan filled with cold water, salt, and black pepper, and place it over medium-high heat.
2. Cook the quinoa to a boil, then reduce the heat, cover, and cook for 20 minutes on a simmer.
3. Fluff and mix the cooked quinoa with a fork and remove it from the heat.
4. Spread the quinoa in a baking stay.
5. Mix eggs, oats, onion, herbs, cheese, salt, and black pepper.
6. Stir in quinoa, then mix well. Make 4 patties out of this quinoa cheese mixture.
7. Divide the patties in the two crisper plates and spray them with cooking oil.

8. Return the crisper plates to the Ninja Foodi Dual Zone Air Fryer.

9. Choose the Air Fry mode for Zone 1 and set the temperature to 390 degrees F and the time to 13 minutes.

10. Select the "MATCH" button to copy the settings for Zone 2.

11. Initiate cooking by pressing the START/STOP button.

12. Flip the patties once cooked halfway through, and resume cooking.

13. Meanwhile, prepare the cucumber yogurt dill sauce by mixing all of its ingredients in a mixing bowl.

14. Place each quinoa patty in a burger bun along with arugula leaves.

15. Serve with yogurt dill sauce.

Nutrition Info:

- (Per serving) Calories 231 | Fat 9g |Sodium 271mg | Carbs 32.8g | Fiber 6.4g | Sugar 7g | Protein 6.3g

Herb And Lemon Cauliflower

Servings: 4

Cooking Time: 10 Minutes

Ingredients:

- 1 cauliflower head, cut into florets
- 4 tablespoons olive oil
- ¼ cup fresh parsley
- 1 tablespoon fresh rosemary
- 1 tablespoon fresh thyme
- 1 teaspoon lemon zest, grated
- 2 tablespoons lemon juice
- ½ teaspoon salt
- ¼ teaspoon crushed red pepper flakes

Directions:

1. Toss cauliflower with oil, herbs and the rest of the ingredients in a bowl.

2. Divide the seasoned cauliflower in the air fryer baskets.

3. Return the air fryer basket 1 to Zone 1, and basket 2 to Zone 2 of the Ninja Foodi 2-Basket Air Fryer.

4. Choose the "Air Fry" mode for Zone 1 at 350 degrees F and 10 minutes of cooking time.

5. Select the "MATCH COOK" option to copy the settings for Zone 2.

6. Initiate cooking by pressing the START/PAUSE BUTTON.

7. Serve warm.

Nutrition Info:

- (Per serving) Calories 212 | Fat 11.8g |Sodium 321mg | Carbs 24.6g | Fiber 4.4g | Sugar 8g | Protein 7.3g

Delicious Potatoes & Carrots

Servings: 8

Cooking Time: 25 Minutes

Ingredients:

- 453g carrots, sliced
- 2 tsp smoked paprika
- 21g sugar
- 30ml olive oil
- 453g potatoes, diced
- ¼ tsp thyme
- ½ tsp dried oregano
- 1 tsp garlic powder
- Pepper
- Salt

Directions:

1. In a bowl, toss carrots and potatoes with 1 tablespoon of oil.

2. Insert a crisper plate in the Ninja Foodi air fryer baskets.

3. Add carrots and potatoes to both baskets.

4. Select zone 1 then select "air fry" mode and set the temperature to 390 degrees F for 15 minutes. Press "match" to match zone 2 settings to zone 1. Press "start/stop" to begin.

5. In a mixing bowl, add cooked potatoes, carrots, smoked paprika, sugar, oil, thyme, oregano, garlic powder, pepper, and salt and toss well.

6. Return carrot and potato mixture into the air fryer basket and cook for 10 minutes more.

Nutrition Info:

- (Per serving) Calories 101 | Fat 3.6g |Sodium 62mg | Carbs 16.6g | Fiber 3g | Sugar 5.1g | Protein 1.6g

Green Beans With Baked Potatoes

Servings:2

Cooking Time:45

Ingredients:

- 2 cups of green beans
- 2 large potatoes, cubed
- 3 tablespoons of olive oil
- 1 teaspoon of seasoned salt
- ½ teaspoon chili powder
- 1/6 teaspoon garlic powder
- 1/4 teaspoon onion powder

Directions:

1. Take a large bowl and pour olive oil into it.

2. Now add all the seasoning in the olive oil and whisk it well.

3. Toss the green bean in it, then transfer it to zone 1 basket of the air fryer.

4. Now season the potatoes with the seasoning and add them to the zone 2 basket.

5. Now set the zone one basket to AIRFRY mode at 350 degrees F for 18 minutes.

6. Now hit 2 for the second basket and set it to AIR FRY mode at 350 degrees F, for 45 minutes.

7. Once the cooking cycle is complete, take out and serve it by transferring it to the serving plates.

Nutrition Info:

- (Per serving) Calories473 | Fat21.6g Sodium796 mg | Carbs 66.6g | Fiber12.9 g | Sugar6 g | Protein8.4 g

Cheesy Potatoes With Asparagus

Servings:2
Cooking Time:35

Ingredients:

- 1-1/2 pounds of russet potato, wedges or cut in half
- 2 teaspoons mixed herbs
- 2 teaspoons chili flakes
- 2 cups asparagus
- 1 cup chopped onion
- 1 tablespoon Dijon mustard
- 1/4 cup fresh cream
- 1 teaspoon olive oil
- 2 tablespoons of butter
- 1/2 teaspoon salt and black pepper
- Water as required
- 1/2 cup Parmesan cheese

Directions:

1. Take a bowl and add asparagus and sweet potato wedges to it.

2. Season it with salt, black pepper, and olive oil.

3. Now add the potato wedges to the zone 1 air fryer basket and asparagus to the zone 2 basket.

4. Set basket1 to AIRFRY mode at 390 degrees F for 12 minutes.

5. Set the zone 2 basket at 390 degrees F, for 30-35 minutes.

6. Meanwhile, take a skillet and add butter and sauté onion in it for a few minutes.

7. Then add salt and Dijon mustard and chili flakes, Parmesan cheese, and fresh cream.

8. Once the air fry mode is done, take out the potato and asparagus.

9. Drizzle the skillet ingredients over the potatoes and serve with asparagus.

Nutrition Info:

- (Per serving) Calories 251| Fat11g | Sodium 279mg | Carbs 31.1g | Fiber 5g | Sugar 4.1g | Protein9 g

Balsamic-glazed Tofu With Roasted Butternut Squash

Servings:4
Cooking Time: 40 Minutes

Ingredients:

- FOR THE BALSAMIC TOFU
- 2 tablespoons balsamic vinegar
- 1 tablespoon maple syrup
- 1 teaspoon soy sauce
- 1 teaspoon Dijon mustard
- 1 (14-ounce) package firm tofu, drained and cut into large cubes
- 1 tablespoon canola oil
- FOR THE BUTTERNUT SQUASH
- 1 small butternut squash
- 1 tablespoon canola oil
- 1 teaspoon light brown sugar
- ¼ teaspoon kosher salt
- ¼ teaspoon freshly ground black pepper

Directions:

1. To prep the balsamic tofu: In a large bowl, whisk together the vinegar, maple syrup, soy sauce, and mustard. Add the tofu and stir to coat. Cover and marinate for at least 20 minutes (or up to overnight in the refrigerator).

2. To prep the butternut squash: Peel the squash and cut in half lengthwise. Remove and discard the seeds. Cut the squash crosswise into ½-inch-thick slices.

3. Brush the squash pieces with the oil, then sprinkle with the brown sugar, salt, and black pepper.

4. To cook the tofu and squash: Install a crisper plate in each of the two baskets. Place the tofu in the Zone 1 basket, drizzle with the oil, and insert the basket in the unit. Place the squash in the Zone 2 basket and insert the basket in the unit.

5. Select Zone 1, select AIR FRY, set the temperature to 400°F, and set the timer to 10 minutes.

6. Select Zone 2, select ROAST, set the temperature to 400°F, and set the timer to 40 minutes. Select SMART FINISH.

7. Press START/PAUSE to begin cooking.

8. When cooking is complete, the tofu will have begun to crisp and brown around the edges and the squash should be tender. Serve hot.

Nutrition Info:

- (Per serving) Calories: 253; Total fat: 11g; Saturated fat: 1g; Carbohydrates: 30g; Fiber: 4.5g; Protein: 11g; Sodium: 237mg

Bacon Wrapped Corn Cob

Servings: 4

Cooking Time: 10 Minutes

Ingredients:

- 4 trimmed corns on the cob
- 8 bacon slices

Directions:

1. Wrap the corn cobs with two bacon slices.
2. Place the wrapped cobs into the Ninja Foodi 2 Baskets Air Fryer baskets.
3. Return the air fryer basket 1 to Zone 1, and basket 2 to Zone 2 of the Ninja Foodi 2-Basket Air Fryer.
4. Choose the "Air Fry" mode for Zone 1 and set the temperature to 355 degrees F and 10 minutes of cooking time.
5. Select the "MATCH COOK" option to copy the settings for Zone 2.
6. Initiate cooking by pressing the START/PAUSE BUTTON.
7. Flip the corn cob once cooked halfway through.
8. Serve warm.

Nutrition Info:

- (Per serving) Calories 350 | Fat 2.6g |Sodium 358mg | Carbs 64.6g | Fiber 14.4g | Sugar 3.3g | Protein 19.9g

Sweet Potatoes & Brussels Sprouts

Servings: 8

Cooking Time: 35 Minutes

Ingredients:

- 340g sweet potatoes, cubed
- 30ml olive oil
- 150g onion, cut into pieces
- 352g Brussels sprouts, halved
- Pepper
- Salt
- For glaze:
- 78ml ketchup
- 115ml balsamic vinegar
- 15g mustard
- 29 ml honey

Directions:

1. In a bowl, toss Brussels sprouts, oil, onion, sweet potatoes pepper, and salt.
2. Insert a crisper plate in the Ninja Foodi air fryer baskets.
3. Add Brussels sprouts and sweet potato mixture in both baskets.
4. Select zone 1, then select "air fry" mode and set the temperature to 390 degrees F for 25 minutes. Press "match" to match zone 2 settings to zone 1. Press "start/stop" to begin. Stir halfway through.
5. Meanwhile, add vinegar, ketchup, honey, and mustard to a saucepan and cook over medium heat for 5-10 minutes.
6. Toss cooked sweet potatoes and Brussels sprouts with sauce.

Nutrition Info:

- (Per serving) Calories 142 | Fat 4.2g |Sodium 147mg | Carbs 25.2g | Fiber 4g | Sugar 8.8g | Protein 2.9g

Desserts Recipes

S'mores Dip With Cinnamon-sugar Tortillas

Servings:4
Cooking Time: 5 Minutes
Ingredients:
- FOR THE S'MORES DIP
- ½ cup chocolate-hazelnut spread
- ¼ cup milk chocolate or white chocolate chips
- ¼ cup graham cracker crumbs
- ½ cup mini marshmallows
- FOR THE CINNAMON-SUGAR TORTILLAS
- 4 (6-inch) flour tortillas
- Butter-flavored cooking spray
- 1 teaspoon granulated sugar
- ½ teaspoon ground cinnamon
- ¼ teaspoon ground cardamom (optional)

Directions:
1. To prep the s'mores dip: Spread the chocolate-hazelnut spread in the bottom of a shallow ovenproof ramekin or dish.
2. Scatter the chocolate chips and graham cracker crumbs over the top. Arrange the marshmallows in a single layer on top of the crumbs.
3. To prep the tortillas: Spray both sides of each tortilla with cooking spray. Cut each tortilla into 8 wedges and sprinkle both sides evenly with sugar, cinnamon, and cardamom (if using).
4. To cook the dip and tortillas: Install a crisper plate in each of the two baskets. Place the ramekin in the Zone 1 basket and insert the basket in the unit. Place the tortillas in the Zone 2 basket and insert the basket in the unit.
5. Select Zone 1, select BAKE, set the temperature to 330°F, and set the timer to 5 minutes.
6. Select Zone 2, select AIR FRY, set the temperature to 375°F, and set the timer to 5 minutes. Select SMART FINISH.
7. Press START/PAUSE to begin cooking.
8. When the Zone 2 timer reads 3 minutes, press START/PAUSE. Remove the basket and shake it to redistribute the chips. Reinsert the basket and press START/PAUSE to resume cooking.
9. When cooking is complete, the dip will be bubbling and golden brown and the chips crispy.
10. If desired, toast the marshmallows more: Select Zone 1, select AIR BROIL, set the temperature to 450°F, and set the timer to 1 minute. Cook until the marshmallows are deep golden brown.
11. Let the dip cool for 2 to 3 minutes. Serve with the cinnamon-sugar tortilla chips.

Nutrition Info:
- (Per serving) Calories: 404; Total Fat: 18g; Saturated fat: 7g; Carbohydrates: 54g; Fiber: 2.5g; Protein: 6g; Sodium: 346mg

Lemony Sweet Twists

Servings:2
Cooking Time:9
Ingredients:
- 1 box store-bought puff pastry
- ½ teaspoon lemon zest
- 1 tablespoon of lemon juice
- 2 teaspoons brown sugar
- Salt, pinch
- 2 tablespoons Parmesan cheese, freshly grated

Directions:
1. Put the puff pastry dough on a clean work area.
2. In a bowl, combine Parmesan cheese, brown sugar, salt, lemon zest, and lemon juice.
3. Press this mixture on both sides of the dough.
4. Now, cut the pastry into 1" x 4" strips.
5. Twist each of the strips.
6. Transfer to both the air fryer baskets.
7. Select zone 1 to air fry mode at 400 degrees F for 9-10 minutes.
8. Select match for zone 2 basket.
9. Once cooked, serve and enjoy.

Nutrition Info:
- (Per serving) Calories 156| Fat10g| Sodium 215mg | Carbs 14g | Fiber 0.4g | Sugar3.3 g | Protein 2.8g

Oreo Rolls

Servings: 9
Cooking Time: 8 Minutes.
Ingredients:
- 1 crescent sheet roll
- 9 Oreo cookies
- Cinnamon powder, to serve
- Powdered sugar, to serve

Directions:
1. Spread the crescent sheet roll and cut it into 9 equal squares.
2. Place one cookie at the center of each square.
3. Wrap each square around the cookies and press the ends to seal.
4. Place half of the wrapped cookies in each crisper plate.
5. Return the crisper plates to the Ninja Foodi Dual Zone Air Fryer.

6. Select the Bake mode for Zone 1 and set the temperature to 360 degrees F and the time to 4-6 minutes.

7. Select the "MATCH" button to copy the settings for Zone 2.

8. Initiate cooking by pressing the START/STOP button.

9. Check for the doneness of the cookie rolls if they are golden brown, else cook 1-2 minutes more.

10. Garnish the rolls with sugar and cinnamon.

11. Serve.

Nutrition Info:

• (Per serving) Calories 175 | Fat 13.1g |Sodium 154mg | Carbs 14g | Fiber 0.8g | Sugar 8.9g | Protein 0.7g

Baked Apples

Servings: 4

Cooking Time: 15 Minutes

Ingredients:

• 4 apples
• 6 teaspoons raisins
• 2 teaspoons chopped walnuts
• 2 teaspoons honey
• ½ teaspoon cinnamon

Directions:

1. Chop off the head of the apples and scoop out the flesh from the center.

2. Stuff the apples with raisins, walnuts, honey and cinnamon.

3. Place these apples in the air fryer basket 1.

4. Return the air fryer basket 1 to Zone 1 of the Ninja Foodi 2-Basket Air Fryer.

5. Choose the "Air Fry" mode for Zone 1 and set the temperature to 350 degrees F and 15 minutes of cooking time.

6. Initiate cooking by pressing the START/PAUSE BUTTON.

7. Serve.

Nutrition Info:

• (Per serving) Calories 175 | Fat 13.1g |Sodium 154mg | Carbs 14g | Fiber 0.8g | Sugar 8.9g | Protein 0.7g

Victoria Sponge Cake

Servings: 8

Cooking Time: 16 Minutes

Ingredients:

• Sponge Cake Ingredients
• 400g self-rising flour
• 450g caster sugar
• 50g lemon curd
• 200g butter
• 4 medium eggs
• 1 tablespoon vanilla essence
• 480ml skimmed milk

• 1 tablespoon olive oil
• 4 tablespoons strawberry jam
• Strawberry buttercream
• 115g butter
• 210g icing sugar
• ½ teaspoon strawberry food coloring
• 1 tablespoon single cream
• 1 teaspoon vanilla essence
• 1 teaspoon maple syrup

Directions:

1. Mix sugar and butter in a bowl using a hand mixer.

2. Beat eggs with oil, and vanilla in a bowl with the mixer until creamy.

3. Stir in milk, flour and curd then mix well.

4. Add butter mixture then mix well.

5. Divide this mixture in two 4 inches greased cake pans.

6. Place one pan in each air fryer basket.

7. Return the air fryer basket 1 to Zone 1, and basket 2 to Zone 2 of the Ninja Foodi 2-Basket Air Fryer.

8. Choose the "Air Fry" mode for Zone 1 and set the temperature to 375 degrees F and 16 minutes of cooking time.

9. Select the "MATCH COOK" option to copy the settings for Zone 2.

10. Initiate cooking by pressing the START/PAUSE BUTTON.

11. Meanwhile, blend the buttercream ingredients in a mixer until fluffy.

12. Place one cake on a plate and top it with the buttercream.

13. Top it jam and then with the other cake.

14. Serve.

Nutrition Info:

• (Per serving) Calories 284 | Fat 16g |Sodium 252mg | Carbs 31.6g | Fiber 0.9g | Sugar 6.6g | Protein 3.7g

Apple Hand Pies

Servings: 8

Cooking Time: 21 Minutes.

Ingredients:

• 8 tablespoons butter, softened
• 12 tablespoons brown sugar
• 2 teaspoons cinnamon, ground
• 4 medium Granny Smith apples, diced
• 2 teaspoons cornstarch
• 4 teaspoons cold water
• 1 (14-oz) package pastry, 9-inch crust pie
• Cooking spray
• 1 tablespoon grapeseed oil
• ½ cup powdered sugar
• 2 teaspoons milk

Directions:

1. Toss apples with brown sugar, butter, and cinnamon in a suitable skillet.
2. Place the skillet over medium heat and stir cook for 5 minutes.
3. Mix cornstarch with cold water in a small bowl.
4. Add cornstarch mixture into the apple and cook for 1 minute until it thickens.
5. Remove this filling from the heat and allow it to cool.
6. Unroll the pie crust and spray on a floured surface.
7. Cut the dough into 16 equal rectangles.
8. Wet the edges of the 8 rectangles with water and divide the apple filling at the center of these rectangles.
9. Place the other 8 rectangles on top and crimp the edges with a fork, then make 2-3 slashes on top.
10. Place 4 small pies in each of the crisper plate.
11. Return the crisper plate to the Ninja Foodi Dual Zone Air Fryer.
12. Choose the Air Fry mode for Zone 1 and set the temperature to 390 degrees F and the time to 17 minutes.
13. Select the "MATCH" button to copy the settings for Zone 2.
14. Initiate cooking by pressing the START/STOP button.
15. Flip the pies once cooked halfway through, and resume cooking.
16. Meanwhile, mix sugar with milk.
17. Pour this mixture over the apple pies.
18. Serve fresh.

Nutrition Info:

- (Per serving) Calories 284 | Fat 16g Sodium 252mg | Carbs 31.6g | Fiber 0.9g | Sugar 6.6g | Protein 3.7g

Chocó Lava Cake

Servings: 4
Cooking Time: 10 Minutes
Ingredients:

- 3 eggs
- 3 egg yolks
- 70g dark chocolate, chopped
- 168g cups powdered sugar
- 96g all-purpose flour
- 1 tsp vanilla
- 113g butter
- ½ tsp salt

Directions:

1. Add chocolate and butter to a bowl and microwave for 30 seconds. Remove from oven and stir until smooth.
2. Add eggs, egg yolks, sugar, flour, vanilla, and salt into the melted chocolate and stir until well combined
3. Pour batter into the four greased ramekins.
4. Insert a crisper plate in Ninja Foodi air fryer baskets.
5. Place ramekins in both baskets.

6. Select zone 1 then select "air fry" mode and set the temperature to 390 degrees F for 10 minutes. Press "match" to match zone 2 settings to zone 1. Press "start/stop" to begin.

Nutrition Info:

- (Per serving) Calories 687 | Fat 37.3g |Sodium 527mg | Carbs 78.3g | Fiber 1.5g | Sugar 57.4g | Protein 10.7g

Fried Oreos

Servings: 8
Cooking Time: 8 Minutes
Ingredients:

- 1 can Pillsbury Crescent Dough (or equivalent)
- 8 Oreo cookies
- 1–2 tablespoons powdered sugar

Directions:

1. Open the crescent dough up and cut it into the right-size pieces to completely wrap each cookie.
2. Wrap each Oreo in dough. Make sure that there are no air bubbles and that the cookies are completely covered.
3. Install a crisper plate in both drawers. Place half the Oreo cookies in the zone 1 drawer and half in zone 2's. Sprinkle the tops with the powdered sugar, then insert the drawers into the unit.
4. Select zone 1, select AIR FRY, set temperature to 390 degrees F/ 200 degrees C, and set time to 8 minutes. Select MATCH to match zone 2 settings to zone 1. Press the START/STOP button to begin cooking.
5. Serve warm and enjoy!

Nutrition Info:

- (Per serving) Calories 338 | Fat 21.2g | Sodium 1503mg | Carbs 5.1g | Fiber 0.3g | Sugar 4.6g | Protein 29.3g

Brownie Muffins

Servings: 10
Cooking Time: 15 Minutes
Ingredients:

- 2 eggs
- 96g all-purpose flour
- 1 tsp vanilla
- 130g powdered sugar
- 25g cocoa powder
- 37g pecans, chopped
- 1 tsp cinnamon
- 113g butter, melted

Directions:

1. In a bowl, whisk eggs, vanilla, butter, sugar, and cinnamon until well mixed.
2. Add cocoa powder and flour and stir until well combined.
3. Add pecans and fold well.
4. Pour batter into the silicone muffin moulds.
5. Insert a crisper plate in Ninja Foodi air fryer baskets.

6. Place muffin moulds in both baskets.

7. Select zone 1, then select "bake" mode and set the temperature to 360 degrees F for 15 minutes. Press "match" and then "start/stop" to begin.

Nutrition Info:

*   (Per serving) Calories 210 | Fat 10.5g |Sodium 78mg | Carbs 28.7g | Fiber 1g | Sugar 20.2g | Protein 2.6g

Apple Crisp

Servings: 8

Cooking Time: 14 Minutes.

Ingredients:

*   3 cups apples, chopped
*   1 tablespoon pure maple syrup
*   2 teaspoons lemon juice
*   3 tablespoons all-purpose flour
*   ⅓ cup quick oats
*   ¼ cup brown sugar
*   2 tablespoons light butter, melted
*   ½ teaspoon cinnamon

Directions:

1. Toss the chopped apples with 1 tablespoon of all-purpose flour, cinnamon, maple syrup, and lemon juice in a suitable bowl.

2. Divide the apples in the two air fryer baskets with their crisper plates.

3. Whisk oats, brown sugar, and remaining all-purpose flour in a small bowl.

4. Stir in melted butter, then divide this mixture over the apples.

5. Return the crisper plate to the Ninja Foodi Dual Zone Air Fryer.

6. Select the Bake mode for Zone 1 and set the temperature to 375 degrees F and the time to 14 minutes.

7. Select the "MATCH" button to copy the settings for Zone 2.

8. Initiate cooking by pressing the START/STOP button.

9. Enjoy fresh.

Nutrition Info:

*   (Per serving) Calories 258 | Fat 12.4g |Sodium 79mg | Carbs 34.3g | Fiber 1g | Sugar 17g | Protein 3.2g

Dessert Empanadas

Servings: 12

Cooking Time: 10 Minutes

Ingredients:

*   12 empanada wrappers thawed
*   2 apples, chopped
*   2 tablespoons raw honey
*   1 teaspoon vanilla extract
*   1 teaspoon cinnamon

*   ⅛ teaspoon nutmeg
*   2 teaspoons cornstarch
*   1 teaspoon water
*   1 egg beaten

Directions:

1. Mix apples with vanilla, honey, nutmeg, and cinnamon in a saucepan.

2. Cook for 3 minutes then mix cornstarch with water and pour into the pan.

3. Cook for 30 seconds.

4. Allow this filling to cool and keep it aside.

5. Spread the wrappers on the working surface.

6. Divide the apple filling on top of the wrappers.

7. Fold the wrappers in half and seal the edges by pressing them.

8. Brush the empanadas with the beaten egg and place them in the air fryer basket 1.

9. Return the air fryer basket 1 to Zone 1 of the Ninja Foodi 2-Basket Air Fryer.

10. Choose the "Air Fry" mode for Zone 1 at 400 degrees F and 10 minutes of cooking time.

11. Initiate cooking by pressing the START/PAUSE BUTTON.

12. Flip the empanadas once cooked halfway through.

13. Serve.

Nutrition Info:

*   (Per serving) Calories 204 | Fat 9g |Sodium 91mg | Carbs 27g | Fiber 2.4g | Sugar 15g | Protein 1.3g

Chocolate Chip Cake

Servings:4

Cooking Time:15

Ingredients:

*   Salt, pinch
*   2 eggs, whisked
*   ½ cup brown sugar
*   ½ cup butter, melted
*   10 tablespoons of almond milk
*   ¼ teaspoon of vanilla extract
*   ½ teaspoon of baking powder
*   1 cup all-purpose flour
*   1 cup of chocolate chips
*   ½ cup of cocoa powder

Directions:

1. Take 2 round baking pan that fits inside the baskets of the air fryer.

2. layer it with baking paper, cut it to the size of a baking pan.

3. In a bowl, whisk the egg, brown sugar, butter, almond milk, and vanilla extract.

4. Whisk it all very well with an electric hand beater.

5. In a second bowl, mix the flour, cocoa powder, baking powder, and salt.

6. Now, mix the dry ingredients slowly with the wet ingredients.

7. Now, at the end fold in the chocolate chips.

8. Incorporate all the ingredients well.

9. Divide this batter into the round baking pan.

10. Set the time for zone 1 to 16 minutes at 350 degrees F at AIR FRY mode.

11. Select the MATCH button for the zone 2 baskets.

12. Check if not done, and let it AIR FRY for one more minute.

13. Once it is done, serve.

Nutrition Info:

- (Per serving) Calories 736| Fat45.5g| Sodium 356mg | Carbs 78.2g | Fiber 6.1g | Sugar 32.7g | Protein11.5 g

Chocolate Cookies

Servings: 18
Cooking Time: 7 Minutes

Ingredients:

- 96g flour
- 57g butter, softened
- 15ml milk
- 7.5g cocoa powder
- 80g chocolate chips
- ½ tsp vanilla
- 35g sugar
- ¼ tsp baking soda
- Pinch of salt

Directions:

1. In a bowl, mix flour, cocoa powder, sugar, baking soda, vanilla, butter, milk, and salt until well combined.

2. Add chocolate chips and mix well.

3. Insert a crisper plate in Ninja Foodi air fryer baskets.

4. Make cookies from the mixture and place in both baskets.

5. Select zone 1 then select "air fry" mode and set the temperature to 360 degrees F for 7 minutes. Press "match" to match zone 2 settings to zone 1. Press "start/stop" to begin.

Nutrition Info:

- (Per serving) Calories 82 | Fat 4.1g |Sodium 47mg | Carbs 10.7g | Fiber 0.4g | Sugar 6.2g | Protein 1g

Apple Fritters

Servings: 14
Cooking Time: 10 Minutes

Ingredients:

- 2 large apples
- 2 cups all-purpose flour
- ½ cup granulated sugar
- 1 tablespoon baking powder
- 1 teaspoon salt
- 1 teaspoon ground cinnamon
- ½ teaspoon ground nutmeg
- ¼ teaspoon ground cloves
- ¾ cup apple cider or apple juice
- 2 eggs
- 3 tablespoons butter, melted
- 1 teaspoon vanilla extract
- For the apple cider glaze:
- 2 cups powdered sugar
- ¼ cup apple cider or apple juice
- ½ teaspoon ground cinnamon
- ¼ teaspoon ground nutmeg

Directions:

1. Peel and core the apples, then cut them into ¼-inch cubes. Spread the apple chunks out on a kitchen towel to absorb any excess moisture.

2. In a mixing bowl, combine the flour, sugar, baking powder, salt, and spices.

3. Add the apple chunks and combine well.

4. Whisk together the apple cider, eggs, melted butter, and vanilla in a small bowl.

5. Combine the wet and dry ingredients in a large mixing bowl.

6. Install a crisper plate in both drawers. Use an ice cream scoop to scoop 3 to 4 dollops of fritter dough into the zone 1 drawer and 3 to 4 dollops into the zone 2 drawer. Insert the drawers into the unit. You may need to cook in batches.

7. Select zone 1, select BAKE, set temperature to 390 degrees F/ 200 degrees C, and set time to 10 minutes. Select MATCH to match zone 2 settings to zone 1. Press the START/STOP button to begin cooking.

8. Meanwhile, make the glaze: Whisk the powdered sugar, apple cider, and spices together until smooth.

9. When the fritters are cooked, drizzle the glaze over them. Let sit for 10 minutes until the glaze sets.

Nutrition Info:

- (Per serving) Calories 221 | Fat 3g | Sodium 288mg | Carbs 46g | Fiber 2g | Sugar 29g | Protein 3g

Strawberry Shortcake

Servings: 8
Cooking Time: 9 Minutes

Ingredients:

- Strawberry topping
- 1-pint strawberries sliced
- ½ cup confectioner's sugar substitute
- Shortcake
- 2 cups Carbquick baking biscuit mix
- ¼ cup butter cold, cubed

- ½ cup confectioner's sugar substitute
- Pinch salt
- ⅔ cup water
- Garnish: sugar free whipped cream

Directions:

1. Mix the shortcake ingredients in a bowl until smooth.
2. Divide the dough into 6 biscuits.
3. Place the biscuits in the air fryer basket 1.
4. Return the air fryer basket 1 to Zone 1 of the Ninja Foodi 2-Basket Air Fryer.
5. Choose the "Air Fry" mode for Zone 1 and set the temperature 400 degrees F and 9 minutes of cooking time.
6. Initiate cooking by pressing the START/PAUSE BUTTON.
7. Mix strawberries with sugar in a saucepan and cook until the mixture thickens.
8. Slice the biscuits in half and add strawberry sauce in between two halves of a biscuit.
9. Serve.

Nutrition Info:

- (Per serving) Calories 157 | Fat 1.3g |Sodium 27mg | Carbs 1.3g | Fiber 1g | Sugar 2.2g | Protein 8.2g

Fudge Brownies

Servings:4

Cooking Time:16

Ingredients:

- 1/2 cup all-purpose flour
- 1/4 cup unsweetened cocoa powder
- 3/4 teaspoon kosher salt
- 2 large eggs, whisked
- 1 tablespoon almond milk
- 1/2 cup brown sugar
- 1/2 cup packed white sugar
- 1/2 tablespoon vanilla extract
- 8 ounces of semisweet chocolate chips, melted
- 2/4 cup unsalted butter, melted

Directions:

1. Take a medium bowl, and use a hand beater to whisk together eggs, milk, both the sugars and vanilla.
2. In a separate microwave-safe bowl, mix melted butter and chocolate and microwave it for 30 seconds to melt the chocolate.
3. Add all the listed dry ingredients to the chocolate mixture.
4. Now incorporate the egg bowl ingredient into the batter.
5. Spray a reasonable size round baking pan that fits in baskets of air fryer
6. Grease the pan with cooking spray.
7. Now pour the batter into the pan, put the crisper plate in baskets.
8. Add the pans and insert the basket into the unit.

9. Select the AIR FRY mode and adjust the setting the temperature to 300 degrees F, for 30 minutes.
10. Check it after 35 minutes and if not done, cook for 10 more minutes
11. Once it's done, take it out and let it get cool before serving.
12. Enjoy.

Nutrition Info:

- (Per serving) Calories 760| Fat43.3 g| Sodium644 mg | Carbs 93.2g | Fiber5.3 g | Sugar 70.2g | Protein 6.2g

Walnut Baklava Bites Pistachio Baklava Bites

Servings:12

Cooking Time: 10 Minutes

Ingredients:

- FOR THE WALNUT BAKLAVA BITES
- ¼ cup finely chopped walnuts
- 2 teaspoons cold unsalted butter, grated
- 2 teaspoons granulated sugar
- ½ teaspoon ground cinnamon
- 6 frozen phyllo shells (from a 1.9-ounce package), thawed
- FOR THE PISTACHIO BAKLAVA BITES
- ¼ cup finely chopped pistachios
- 2 teaspoons very cold unsalted butter, grated
- 2 teaspoons granulated sugar
- ¼ teaspoon ground cardamom (optional)
- 6 frozen phyllo shells (from a 1.9-ounce package), thawed
- FOR THE HONEY SYRUP
- ¼ cup hot water
- ¼ cup honey
- 2 teaspoons fresh lemon juice

Directions:

1. To prep the walnut baklava bites: In a small bowl, combine the walnuts, butter, sugar, and cinnamon. Spoon the filling into the phyllo shells.
2. To prep the pistachio baklava bites: In a small bowl, combine the pistachios, butter, sugar, and cardamom (if using). Spoon the filling into the phyllo shells.
3. To cook the baklava bites: Install a crisper plate in each of the two baskets. Place the walnut baklava bites in the Zone 1 basket and insert the basket in the unit. Place the pistachio baklava bites in the Zone 2 basket and insert the basket in the unit.
4. Select Zone 1, select BAKE, set the temperature to 330°F, and set the timer to 10 minutes. Press MATCH COOK to match Zone 2 settings to Zone 1.
5. Press START/PAUSE to begin cooking.
6. When cooking is complete, the shells will be golden brown and crisp.

7. To make the honey syrup: In a small bowl, whisk together the hot water, honey, and lemon juice. Dividing evenly, pour the syrup over the baklava bites (you may hear a crackling sound).

8. Let cool completely before serving, about 1 hour.

Nutrition Info:

- (Per serving) Calories: 262; Total fat: 16g; Saturated fat: 3g; Carbohydrates: 29g; Fiber: 1g; Protein: 2g; Sodium: 39mg

Cinnamon Sugar Dessert Fries

Servings: 4

Cooking Time: 15 Minutes

Ingredients:

- 2 sweet potatoes
- 1 tablespoon butter, melted
- 1 teaspoon butter, melted
- 2 tablespoons sugar
- ½ teaspoon ground cinnamon

Directions:

1. Peel and cut the sweet potatoes into skinny fries.

2. Coat the fries with 1 tablespoon of butter.

3. Install a crisper plate into each drawer. Place half the sweet potatoes in the zone 1 drawer and half in zone 2's, then insert the drawers into the unit.

4. Select zone 1, select AIR FRY, set temperature to 390 degrees F/ 200 degrees C, and set time to 15 minutes. Select MATCH to match zone 2 settings to zone 1. Press the START/STOP button to begin cooking.

5. When the time reaches 11 minutes, press START/STOP to pause the unit. Remove the drawers and flip the fries. Re-insert the drawers into the unit and press START/STOP to resume cooking.

6. Meanwhile, mix the 1 teaspoon of butter, the sugar, and the cinnamon in a large bowl.

7. When the fries are done, add them to the bowl, and toss them to coat.

8. Serve and enjoy!

Nutrition Info:

- (Per serving) Calories 110 | Fat 4g | Sodium 51mg | Carbs 18g | Fiber 2g | Sugar 10g | Protein 1g

Zesty Cranberry Scones

Servings: 8

Cooking Time: 16 Minutes.

Ingredients:

- 4 cups of flour
- ½ cup brown sugar
- 2 tablespoons baking powder
- ½ teaspoon ground nutmeg
- ½ teaspoon salt
- ½ cup butter, chilled and diced

- 2 cups fresh cranberry
- ⅔ cup sugar
- 2 tablespoons orange zest
- 1 ¼ cups half and half cream
- 2 eggs

Directions:

1. Whisk flour with baking powder, salt, nutmeg, and both the sugars in a bowl.

2. Stir in egg and cream, mix well to form a smooth dough.

3. Fold in cranberries along with the orange zest.

4. Knead this dough well on a work surface.

5. Cut 3-inch circles out of the dough.

6. Divide the scones in the crisper plates and spray them with cooking oil.

7. Return the crisper plates to the Ninja Foodi Dual Zone Air Fryer.

8. Choose the Air Fry mode for Zone 1 and set the temperature to 375 degrees F and the time to 16 minutes.

9. Select the "MATCH" button to copy the settings for Zone 2.

10. Initiate cooking by pressing the START/STOP button.

11. Flip the scones once cooked halfway and resume cooking.

12. Enjoy!

Nutrition Info:

- (Per serving) Calories 204 | Fat 9g | Sodium 91mg | Carbs 27g | Fiber 2.4g | Sugar 15g | Protein 1.3g

Air Fryer Sweet Twists

Servings:2

Cooking Time:9

Ingredients:

- 1 box store-bought puff pastry
- ½ teaspoon cinnamon
- ½ teaspoon sugar
- ½ teaspoon black sesame seeds
- Salt, pinch
- 2 tablespoons Parmesan cheese, freshly grated

Directions:

1. Place the dough on a work surface.

2. Take a small bowl and mix cheese, sugar, salt, sesame seeds, and cinnamon.

3. Press this mixture on both sides of the dough.

4. Now, cut the pastry into 1" x 3" strips.

5. Twist each of the strips 2 times and then lay it onto the flat.

6. Transfer to both the air fryer baskets.

7. Select zone 1 to air fry mode at 400 degrees F for 9-10 minutes.

8. Select the MATCH button for the zone 2 basket.

9. Once cooked, serve.

Nutrition Info:

- (Per serving) Calories 140| Fat9.4g| Sodium 142mg | Carbs 12.3g | Fiber0.8 g | Sugar 1.2g | Protein 2g

Blueberry Pie Egg Rolls

Servings: 12
Cooking Time: 5 Minutes

Ingredients:

- 12 egg roll wrappers
- 2 cups of blueberries
- 1 tablespoon of cornstarch
- ½ cup of agave nectar
- 1 teaspoon of lemon zest
- 2 tablespoons of water
- 1 tablespoon of lemon juice
- Olive oil or butter flavored cooking spray
- Confectioner's sugar for dusting

Directions:

1. Mix blueberries with cornstarch, lemon zest, agave and water in a saucepan.
2. Cook this mixture for 5 minutes on a simmer.
3. Allow the mixture to cool.
4. Spread the roll wrappers and divide the filling at the center of the wrappers.
5. Fold the two edges and roll each wrapper.
6. Wet and seal the wrappers then place them in the air fryer basket 1.
7. Spray these rolls with cooking spray.
8. Return the air fryer basket 1 to Zone 1 of the Ninja Foodi 2-Basket Air Fryer.
9. Choose the "Air Fry" mode for Zone 1 at 350 degrees F and 5 minutes of cooking time.
10. Initiate cooking by pressing the START/PAUSE BUTTON.
11. Dust the rolls with confectioner' sugar.
12. Serve.

Nutrition Info:

- (Per serving) Calories 258 | Fat 12.4g |Sodium 79mg | Carbs 34.3g | Fiber 1g | Sugar 17g | Protein 3.2g

Grilled Peaches

Servings: 2
Cooking Time: 5 Minutes

Ingredients:

- 2 yellow peaches, peeled and cut into wedges
- ¼ cup graham cracker crumbs
- ¼ cup brown sugar
- ¼ cup butter diced into tiny cubes
- Whipped cream or ice cream

Directions:

1. Toss peaches with crumbs, brown sugar, and butter in a bowl.

2. Spread the peaches in one air fryer basket.
3. Return the air fryer basket to the Ninja Foodi 2 Baskets Air Fryer.
4. Choose the "Air Fry" mode for Zone 1 and set the temperature to 350 degrees F and 5 minutes of cooking time.
5. Initiate cooking by pressing the START/PAUSE BUTTON.
6. Serve the peaches with a scoop of ice cream.

Nutrition Info:

- (Per serving) Calories 327 | Fat 14.2g |Sodium 672mg | Carbs 47.2g | Fiber 1.7g | Sugar 24.8g | Protein 4.4g

Delicious Apple Fritters

Servings: 10
Cooking Time: 8 Minutes

Ingredients:

- 236g Bisquick
- 2 apples, peel & dice
- 158ml milk
- 30ml butter, melted
- 1 tsp cinnamon
- 24g sugar

Directions:

1. In a bowl, mix Bisquick, cinnamon, and sugar.
2. Add milk and mix until dough forms. Add apple and stir well.
3. Insert a crisper plate in Ninja Foodi air fryer baskets.
4. Make fritters from the mixture and place in both baskets. Brush fritters with melted butter.
5. Select zone 1 then select "air fry" mode and set the temperature to 360 degrees F for 10 minutes. Press "match" to match zone 2 settings to zone 1. Press "start/stop" to begin.

Nutrition Info:

- (Per serving) Calories 171 | Fat 6.7g |Sodium 352mg | Carbs 25.8g | Fiber 1.7g | Sugar 10.8g | Protein 2.7g

Biscuit Doughnuts

Servings: 8

Cooking Time: 15 Minutes.

Ingredients:

- ½ cup white sugar
- 1 teaspoon cinnamon
- ½ cup powdered sugar
- 1 can pre-made biscuit dough
- Coconut oil
- Melted butter to brush biscuits

Directions:

1. Place all the biscuits on a cutting board and cut holes in the center of each biscuit using a cookie cutter.
2. Grease the crisper plate with coconut oil.
3. Place the biscuits in the two crisper plates while keeping them 1 inch apart.
4. Return the crisper plates to the Ninja Foodi Dual Zone Air Fryer.
5. Choose the Air Fry mode for Zone 1 and set the temperature to 375 degrees F and the time to 15 minutes.
6. Select the "MATCH" button to copy the settings for Zone 2.
7. Initiate cooking by pressing the START/STOP button.
8. Brush all the donuts with melted butter and sprinkle cinnamon and sugar on top.
9. Air fry these donuts for one minute more.
10. Enjoy!

Nutrition Info:

- (Per serving) Calories 192 | Fat 9.3g |Sodium 133mg | Carbs 27.1g | Fiber 1.4g | Sugar 19g | Protein 3.2g

Bread Pudding

Servings: 4

Cooking Time: 15 Minutes

Ingredients:

- 2 cups bread cubes
- 1 egg
- ⅔ cup heavy cream
- ½ teaspoon vanilla extract
- ¼ cup sugar
- ¼ cup chocolate chips

Directions:

1. Grease two 4 inches baking dish with a cooking spray.
2. Divide the bread cubes in the baking dishes and sprinkle chocolate chips on top.
3. Beat egg with cream, sugar and vanilla in a bowl.
4. Divide this mixture in the baking dishes.
5. Place one pan in each air fryer basket.
6. Return the air fryer basket 1 to Zone 1, and basket 2 to Zone 2 of the Ninja Foodi 2-Basket Air Fryer.
7. Choose the "Air Fry" mode for Zone 1 at 350 degrees F and 15 minutes of cooking time.
8. Select the "MATCH COOK" option to copy the settings for Zone 2.
9. Initiate cooking by pressing the START/PAUSE BUTTON.
10. Allow the pudding to cool and serve.

Nutrition Info:

- (Per serving) Calories 149 | Fat 1.2g |Sodium 3mg | Carbs 37.6g | Fiber 5.8g | Sugar 29g | Protein 1.1g

Appendix : Recipes Index

"fried" Chicken With Warm Baked Potato Salad 25

A

Acorn Squash Slices 52
Air Fried Bacon And Eggs 6
Air Fried Lamb Chops 35
Air Fryer Meatloaves 33
Air Fryer Sausage Patties 14
Air Fryer Sweet Twists 66
Air Fryer Vegetables 52
Almond Chicken 27
Apple Crisp 63
Apple Fritters 64
Apple Hand Pies 61
Avocado Fries With Sriracha Dip 21

B

Bacon Wrapped Corn Cob 59
Bagels 14
Baked Apples 61
Baked Mushroom And Mozzarella Frittata With Breakfast Potatoes 9
Balsamic Duck Breast 30
Balsamic-glazed Tofu With Roasted Butternut Squash 58
Banana And Raisins Muffins 11
Banana Muffins 8
Bang Bang Shrimp 42
Barbecue Chicken Drumsticks With Crispy Kale Chips 27
Beef And Bean Taquitos With Mexican Rice 38
Beef Jerky Pineapple Jerky 18
Beef Kofta Kebab 34
Beef Ribs I 36
Beef Ribs Ii 34
Beer Battered Fish Fillet 44
Bell Peppers With Sausages 33
Biscuit Doughnuts 68
Blueberry Pie Egg Rolls 67
Bread Pudding 68
Breaded Pork Chops 38
Breakfast Bacon 7
Breakfast Cheese Sandwich 13
Breakfast Sausage Omelet 7
Broiled Crab Cakes With Hush Puppies 42
Broiled Teriyaki Salmon With Eggplant In Stir-fry Sauce 46

Brownie Muffins 62
Brussels Sprouts 55
Brussels Sprouts Potato Hash 12
Buffalo Chicken 31
Buffalo Seitan With Crispy Zucchini Noodles 51

C

Cheddar Quiche 22
Cheddar-stuffed Chicken 26
Cheese Corn Fritters 20
Cheese Stuffed Mushrooms 19
Cheesy Baked Eggs 9
Cheesy Potatoes With Asparagus 58
Chicken & Broccoli 25
Chicken And Potatoes 26
Chicken Breast Strips 29
Chicken Caprese 29
Chicken Cordon Bleu 32
Chicken Leg Piece 23
Chicken Potatoes 30
Chicken Tenders 16
Chicken Thighs With Brussels Sprouts 28
Chicken Wings 28
Chickpea Fritters 53
Chili Lime Tilapia 48
Chili-lime Crispy Chickpeas Pizza-seasoned Crispy Chickpeas 22
Chinese Bbq Pork 34
Chocó Lava Cake 62
Chocolate Chip Cake 63
Chocolate Cookies 64
Cinnamon Apple French Toast 6
Cinnamon Sugar Dessert Fries 66
Codfish With Herb Vinaigrette 50
Cornbread 8
Cornish Hen With Asparagus 30
Crab Cake Poppers 21
Crab Cakes 17
Crispy Plantain Chips 15
Crispy Sesame Chicken 24
Crumbed Chicken Katsu 28
Crumb-topped Sole 45
Crusted Shrimp 44

D

Delicious Apple Fritters 67
Delicious Potatoes & Carrots 57
Dessert Empanadas 63

E

Easy Chicken Thighs 27
Egg And Avocado In The Ninja Foodi 8
Egg White Muffins 7
Egg With Baby Spinach 12

F

Fresh Mix Veggies In Air Fryer 52
Fried Artichoke Hearts 53
Fried Asparagus 53
Fried Cheese 21
Fried Lobster Tails 49
Fried Olives 55
Fried Oreos 62
Fried Patty Pan Squash 55
Fried Pickles 17
Fried Tilapia 48
Frozen Breaded Fish Fillet 50
Fudge Brownies 65

G

Garlic Bread 16
Garlic Shrimp With Pasta Alfredo 47
Garlic Sirloin Steak 41
Garlic-rosemary Brussels Sprouts 56
General Tso's Chicken 24
Glazed Scallops 42
Glazed Thighs With French Fries 23
Green Beans With Baked Potatoes 57
Grilled Peaches 67

H

Healthy Air Fried Veggies 54
Healthy Oatmeal Muffins 10
Herb And Lemon Cauliflower 57
Herb Tuna Patties 44
Honey Sriracha Mahi Mahi 49

I

Italian-style Meatballs With Garlicky Roasted Broccoli 37

K

Keto Baked Salmon With Pesto 48
Korean Bbq Beef 33

L

Lamb Chops With Dijon Garlic 40
Lemony Sweet Twists 60

M

Mac And Cheese Balls 20
Miso-glazed Shishito Peppers Charred Lemon Shishito Peppers 18
Mixed Air Fry Veggies 51
Mongolian Beef With Sweet Chili Brussels Sprouts 39
Morning Egg Rolls 13
Mozzarella Balls 19

O

Oreo Rolls 60

P

Parmesan French Fries 17
Parmesan-crusted Fish Sticks With Baked Macaroni And Cheese 46
Pepper Poppers 54
Peppered Asparagus 15
Pork Chops 35
Pork Chops And Potatoes 36
Pork Chops With Apples 38
Pork Chops With Brussels Sprouts 36
Potato Chips 19
Potatoes & Beans 54
Pretzel Chicken Cordon Bleu 29
Pumpkin French Toast Casserole With Sweet And Spicy Twisted Bacon 6

Q

Quiche Breakfast Peppers 10
Quinoa Patties 56

R

Roasted Garlic Chicken Pizza With Cauliflower "wings" 31
Roasted Tomato Bruschetta With Toasty Garlic Bread 15
Rosemary Asparagus & Potatoes 53

S

S'mores Dip With Cinnamon-sugar Tortillas 60
Salmon Nuggets 43
Salmon With Coconut 43
Salmon With Fennel Salad 47
Saucy Carrots 56

Sausage & Butternut Squash 11
Sausage Hash And Baked Eggs 12
Savory Salmon Fillets 48
Scallops With Greens 45
Seafood Shrimp Omelet 49
Smoked Salmon 45
Spicy Salmon Fillets 43
Spinach And Red Pepper Egg Cups With Coffee-glazed Canadian Bacon 10
Spinach Egg Muffins 6
Steak And Asparagus Bundles 41
Steak In Air Fry 35
Strawberries And Walnuts Muffins 20
Strawberry Shortcake 64
Stuffed Bell Peppers 17
Stuffed Mushrooms 16
Sweet Potato Hash 11
Sweet Potatoes & Brussels Sprouts 59

T

Tasty Lamb Patties 40
Tasty Pork Skewers 40
Tater Tots 22
Tender Pork Chops 39
Tomahawk Steak 35
Turkey And Beef Meatballs 37

V

Victoria Sponge Cake 61

W

Walnut Baklava Bites Pistachio Baklava Bites 65
Whole Chicken 26

Y

Yummy Chicken Breasts 23

Z

Zesty Cranberry Scones 66
Zucchini Chips 18

Printed in Great Britain
by Amazon